The Unauthorized Guide to The Fantasy Series A Song of Ice and Fire

SB Jeffrey

The role of the book within our culture is changing. The change is brought on by new ways to acquire & use content, the rapid dissemination of information and real-time peer collaboration on a global scale. Despite these changes one thing is clear--"the book" in it's traditional form continues to play an important role in learning and communication. The book you are holding in your hands utilizes the unique characteristics of the Internet -- relying on web infrastructure and collaborative tools to share and use resources in keeping with the characteristics of the medium (user-created, defying control, etc.)--while maintaining all the convenience and utility of a real book.

Contents

The Series

A Song of Ice and Fire

US covers for the first five books	
A Game of Thrones *A Clash of Kings* *A Storm of Swords* *A Feast for Crows* *A Dance with Dragons* *The Winds of Winter* *A Dream of Spring*	
Author	George R. R. Martin
Country	United States
Language	English
Genre	High fantasy, dark fantasy, historical fantasy
Publisher	Bantam Books (USA) Voyager Books (UK, Australia)
Published	August 6, 1996 – present
Media type	Print (Hardcover and paperback) Audiobook

A Song of Ice and Fire is an award-winning series of epic fantasy novels by American novelist and screenwriter George R. R. Martin. Martin began writing the series in 1991 and the first volume was published in 1996. Originally planned as a trilogy, the series now consists of four published volumes with three more planned. There are also three prequel novellas available, with several more planned, and a series of novellas consisting of excerpts of the main novels. One of these excerpt novellas has won a Hugo Award. The series has been translated into more than twenty languages and the fourth volume reached the top of the *New York Times* bestseller lists upon its release. Overall, the series has sold more than 3.5 million copies in the USA and more than 7 million worldwide.

The story of *A Song of Ice and Fire* takes place in a fictional world, primarily upon a continent called Westeros but also on a large landmass to the east, known as Essos. Most of the characters are human but as the series progresses other races are introduced, such as the cold and menacing Others from the far North and fire-breathing dragons from the East, both races thought to be extinct by the people of the story. There are three principal storylines in the series: the chronicling of a dynastic civil war for control of Westeros between several competing families; the rising threat of the Others who dwell beyond an immense wall of ice that forms Westeros' northern border; and the ambition of Daenerys Targaryen, the exiled daughter of a king who was murdered in another civil war fifteen years previously, to return to Westeros and claim her rightful throne. As the series progresses, all three storylines become increasingly interwoven and dependent on each other.

The series is told in the limited third-person through the eyes of a number of point of view characters. By the end of the fourth volume, there have been seventeen such characters with multiple chapters and eight who only have one chapter apiece.

The growing popularity of the series led to it being optioned by HBO for development of a television adaptation, named *Game of Thrones*. A pilot episode was produced in 2009 and a series commitment for nine further episodes was made in March 2010.

There are board and role-playing games based on the books available, as well as a collection of artwork based on and inspired by the series. The French video game company, Cyanide, has announced that they have partnered with Martin to create a video game adaption of the books, entitled *A Game of Thrones: Genesis*.

The series is the number 1 rated fantasy series at the Internet Book List.

Back story

The background to *A Song of Ice and Fire* is revealed through the lengthy appendices which follow on from each volume, with additional information revealed through the novellas, the text of the novels themselves and the role-playing game.

The narrative is set primarily in the fictional Seven Kingdoms of Westeros, a large, South America–sized continent with an ancient history stretching back some twelve thousand years, and where the seasons last for years. The original inhabitants of the land were the Children of The Forest (whose old gods are still worshiped in the North), a diminutive race who lived in harmony with nature and employed powerful magic. The First Men, a civilization of primitive warriors wielding bronze weapons and riding horses, crossed over from the eastern continent via a land bridge (destroyed in the resulting conflicts) and fought a series of wars against the Children which ended with the Pact of the Isle of Faces being signed, with the First Men taking control of the open lands and the Children remaining in the forests.

The Pact was weakened after four thousand years by the emergence of the Others, an enigmatic race from the furthermost north, who swept south into Westeros and caused great death and destruction, bringing about a night that lasted a generation and a winter that lasted decades. In the War for the Dawn, the Others were thrown back by the First Men and the Children of The Forest, and the vast wall of ice was raised to bar their passage south should they come again. In the following centuries the Children gradually disappeared, and it was presumed that they left Westeros or died out altogether.

Approximately two thousand years after the War for the Dawn, the Andals crossed the narrow sea from the eastern continent. The Andals wielded iron weapons, had tamed horses to use in battle and brought with them the Faith of the Seven. They landed in the Vale of Arryn and over the course of several millennia subjugated the southern kingdoms. However, they could not take the North due to natural defences. Over time six great and powerful kingdoms were forged across Westeros: the Kingdom of the North, the Kingdom of the Iron Islands, the Kingdom of Vale and Sky, the Kingdom of the Rock, the Kingdom of the Storm Kings and the Kingdom of the Reach. A seventh kingdom—that of the Riverlands—was repeatedly conquered by its neighbours and eventually was destroyed altogether, whilst the small desert kingships in the far south of Westeros were divided by constant struggle and war. One thousand years prior to the events of the novels, a great host of refugees from the region of the River Rhoyne on the eastern continent—displaced by the growing power of a distant empire called Valyria—crossed the narrow sea under the warrior-queen Nymeria and landed in the southern-most part of Westeros. The Rhoynar allied with the native Lord Mors Martell and conquered the southern peninsula of Dorne, forging another powerful kingdom.

Five centuries later the expanding Valyrian Freehold had reached the far coast of the narrow sea and established links with Westeros, using the island of Dragonstone as a trading port. However, a mere century later the Valyrian Freehold was destroyed by a titanic disaster known as the Doom. The Valyrian family that controlled Dragonstone, the Targaryens, spent a further century in preparing their forces, and then launched a devastating invasion of Westeros under Aegon the Conqueror. Although their forces were tiny, they had with them the last three dragons in the western world and they were able to use these to subjugate the continent. Six of the Seven Kingdoms were conquered in this initial war, but Dorne resisted so fiercely that Aegon agreed to let them remain independent. The Targaryens adopted the native Faith of the Seven (although they still married brother to sister in the ancient Valyrian tradition in defiance of the Faith's teachings) and Westerosi customs, and within a few decades had crushed all resistance to their rule. Dorne was eventually absorbed through marriage-alliance. The last dragons died out a century and a half into the Targaryen rule, but by this time they had become the ruling power on the continent and their rule was not challenged.

Fifteen years prior to the beginning of the novels, the Targaryens were displaced from power in a civil war brought about by King Aerys II's (called "the Mad King") insanity and cruelty. An alliance of houses under the leadership of Robert Baratheon, Jon Arryn, and Eddard Stark successfully destroyed the Targaryen armies, then went on to kill king Aerys's heirs and wiped out most of the line, aside from Aerys' pregnant wife and his son Viserys, who fled to Dragonstone. King Aerys himself was killed by Jaime Lannister, his own sworn sword, who since then has been nicknamed the Kingslayer. Aerys' wife died giving birth to Daenerys Targaryen, who was taken to safety in the Free Cities beyond the narrow sea by loyal retainers. In the meantime, Robert Baratheon took the Iron Throne and married Cersei

Lannister, whose father Tywin had delivered Robert the capital of King's Landing through treachery.

Synopsis

A Song of Ice and Fire follows three principal storylines, divided by geography and participants.

The first storyline, set in the Seven Kingdoms themselves, chronicles a many-sided struggle for the Iron Throne that develops after King Robert's death. The throne is claimed by his son Joffrey, supported by his mother's powerful family, House Lannister. However, Lord Eddard Stark, King Robert's Hand, finds out Robert's children are illegitimate, and that the throne should therefore fall to Robert's unpopular eldest brother, Stannis. Robert's charismatic and popular youngest brother, Renly, also places a claim, openly disregarding the order of precedence, with the support of the powerful House Tyrell. While the claimants battle for the Iron Throne, Robb Stark, Lord Eddard Stark's heir, is proclaimed King in the North as the northmen and their allies in the Riverlands seek to return to self-rule. Likewise, Balon Greyjoy also (re-)claims the ancient throne of his own region, the Iron Islands, with an eye toward independence. This so-called War of the Five Kings is the principal storyline of the first four novels; indeed, the fourth novel primarily concerns Westeros's recovery from it in the face of the coming winter and the political machinations of those seeking to gain in its aftermath.

The second storyline is set on the extreme northern border of Westeros. Here, many thousands of years ago, a huge wall of ice and gravel was constructed by both magic and labor to defend Westeros from the threat of The Others, a race of now-mythical creatures living in the uttermost north. This Wall, 300 miles (480 km) long and 700 feet (210 m) tall, is defended and maintained by the Sworn Brotherhood of the Night's Watch, whose duty is to guard the kingdom against the Others. By the time of the novels, the Others have not been seen in over 8,000 years, and the Night's Watch has devolved into essentially a penal colony: it is badly under-strength, manned primarily by criminals and refugees with only a few knights or men of honor to stiffen them, and spends most of its time dealing with the human "wildlings" or "free folk" who live beyond the Wall. This storyline is told primarily through the eyes of Jon Snow, bastard son of Eddard Stark, as he rises through the ranks of the Watch, learns the true nature of the threat from the north, and prepares to defend the realm even though the people of Westeros are too busy warring to send support. By the end of the third volume, this storyline is somewhat entangled with the civil war to the south.

The third storyline is set on the huge eastern continent of Essos, across the narrow sea, and follows the adventures of Daenerys Targaryen, the last scion of House Targaryen and another claimant to the Iron Throne. Daenerys's adventures showcase her growing ability as she rises from a pauper sold into a dynastic marriage to a barbarian warlord to a powerful and canny ruler in her own right. Her rise is aided by the birth of three dragons, creatures thought long extinct, from fossilized eggs given to her as wedding gifts. Because her family standard is the dragon, these creatures are of symbolic value before they have grown big enough to be of tactical use. Though her story is separated from the others by many thousands of miles, her stated goal is to reclaim the Iron Throne.

Concept and creation

Background

Martin had a long love of model knights and medieval history, but his early novels and short stories mostly fit into the science fiction genre; however, eventually several fantasy stories did appear, such as *The Ice Dragon*. In the mid-1980s, Martin worked mainly in Hollywood, principally as a writer or producer on *The New Twilight Zone* and *Beauty and the Beast*. After *Beauty and the Beast* ended in 1989 Martin returned to writing prose and started work on a science fiction novel called *Avalon*. In 1991, whilst struggling with this story, Martin conceived of a scene where several youngsters find a dead direwolf with a stag's antler in its throat. The direwolf has several pups, which are taken by the youngsters to raise as their own. Martin's imagination was fired by this idea and he developed it into an epic fantasy story, which he envisaged as a trilogy consisting of the books *A Game of Thrones*, *A Dance with Dragons* and *The Winds of Winter*. Martin had previously apparently not been inspired by the genre, but reading Tad Williams' *Memory, Sorrow, and Thorn* series had convinced him it could be approached in a more adult and mature way than previous authors.

After a hiatus spent producing a television pilot for a series called *Doorways*, Martin resumed work on *A Game of Thrones* in 1994 and completed it the following year, although he was only partway through his initial plan for the first novel. As a result of this, Martin then expanded his plan for the series to four books, and then to six. Publication of *A Game of Thrones* followed in early 1996. Pre-release publicity included publication of a "sample novella" called *Blood of the Dragon*, which went on to win the 1997 Hugo Award for Best Novella. To fit *A Game of Thrones* into one volume, Martin had pulled out the last quarter or so of the book and made it the opening section of the second book, 1998's *A Clash of Kings*. In May 2005 Martin noted that his manuscript for *A Game of Thrones* had been 1088 pages long without the appendices, and *A Clash of Kings* was even longer at 1184 pages.

Influences

Although Martin has acknowledged his debt to the works of J.R.R. Tolkien, Jack Vance and Tad Williams, the series differs from these earlier works in its greater interest in and use of realistic elements. While Tolkien was inspired by mythology, *A Song of Ice and Fire* is more clearly influenced by medieval history, most notably the Wars of the Roses. Likewise, while Tolkien tended toward romantic relationships, Martin writes frankly of sex, including incest, adultery, prostitution, and rape. As a result, illegitimate children play prominent roles throughout the series. This has led to the series being cited as a forerunner of a 'gritty' new wave of epic fantasy authors that followed, including Scott Lynch, Joe Abercrombie, Steven Erikson and Scott Bakker. On his website, Martin has acknowledged historical fiction authors such as Bernard Cornwell and George MacDonald Fraser to be influences on the series. Martin has cited the cover blurb by Robert Jordan for the first book to have been influential in ensuring the series' early success with fantasy readers.

Martin is an avid student of medieval Europe, and has said that the Wars of the Roses, along with many other events in Europe during that time, have influenced the series. However, he insists that "there's really no one-for-one character-for-character correspondence. I like to use history to flavor my fantasy, to add texture and verisimilitude, but simply rewriting history with the names changed has no appeal for me. I prefer to reimagine it all, and take it in new and unexpected directions."

Publication history

#	Title	Pages	Chapters	Earliest Release
1.	*A Game of Thrones*	694	73	August 1996
2.	*A Clash of Kings*	768	70	November 1998
3.	*A Storm of Swords*	973	82	August 2000
4.	*A Feast for Crows*	753	46	October 2005
5.	*A Dance with Dragons*	(Forthcoming)		
6.	*The Winds of Winter*	(Forthcoming)		
7.	*A Dream of Spring*	(Forthcoming)		

All page totals given are for the US hardcover edition.

After expanding the series to four volumes, Martin remarked, "What can I say? It's a BIG story, and a cast of thousands."

After *A Storm of Swords* was completed in 2000, Martin began writing *A Dance with Dragons*, the intended fourth volume which would pick up the story five years after the previous volume. Martin found it difficult to make this work without an over-reliance on flashbacks. At the World Science Fiction Convention in Philadelphia on 1 September 2001, Martin announced that he was scrapping more than a year's work and writing a different fourth book that would fill in the gap, named *A Feast for Crows*. He found it extremely difficult to go back and start again, especially as this novel was not planned for in his scheme for the series, and work on the book progressed slowly.

By May 2005, *A Feast for Crows* had become longer than *A Storm of Swords* (the manuscript for which had been 1521 pages) and Martin's publishers said they could not publish the book in one volume. They suggested splitting the book in two and releasing the volumes as *A Feast for Crows, Volume I* and *A Feast for Crows, Volume II*, but Martin was unhappy with this idea. After discussing the matter with his publishers and his friend and fellow writer Daniel Abraham, Martin decided to split the book by character and location instead. The published *A Feast for Crows* thus contained all of the characters in the South of the Seven Kingdoms, while the forthcoming *A Dance with Dragons* will contain the characters in the North, the Free Cities and in Slaver's Bay.

In a May 2005 statement, the author also said that this move now meant that the series would require seven volumes. Martin recognized that this decision could cause frustration among some of his fans. He wrote: "I know some of you may be disappointed, especially when you buy *A Feast for Crows* and discover that your favorite character does not appear, but given the realities I think this was the best solution... and the more I look at it, the more convinced I am that these two parallel novels, when taken together, will actually tell the story better than one big book."

These problems aside, *A Feast for Crows* was released in October 2005 and immediately won largely positive reviews. *Time* dubbed Martin "the American Tolkien", and the novel went straight to the top of the *New York Times* bestseller list.

Despite initial hopes of *A Dance with Dragons* being published quickly after *A Feast for Crows*, the writing and revision process for this fifth novel proved more difficult than anticipated. On January 1, 2008, Martin published an update on his website saying he hoped to have the book published in the autumn of 2008. As of October 2010, the author has published no further updates on his website. Although major retailers had quoted release dates for *A Dance with Dragons* of September 29, 2009 in the US and the following month in the UK, Martin stated that these release dates were incorrect, and that he would announce the release of *A Dance with Dragons* when he has finished the manuscript. Martin has in the past announced finishing dates for earlier works on his blog, and in the last several years also announced the genesis of other projects, which has caused some fans to wonder if he has lost interest in writing *A Song of Ice and Fire*. Martin has said that this is not the case.[*citation needed*] George R. R. Martin has addressed fan frustration with the many delays in releasing *Ice and Fire* novels, including fears that he may "pull a Robert Jordan" and leave the series forever unfinished. Martin insists that he will not be bullied and continues to work at his own pace, on this and several other projects, to make sure they come out as good as he can possibly make them.Wikipedia:Verifiability In a February 2009 update on his LiveJournal, Martin confirmed that he had hoped to finish the novel in June, which would permit a September-October 2009 publication. This goal was not achieved, though in late June 2009 he mentioned that he had achieved more progress within the preceding weeks than any other concentrated period of work of the previous year, perhaps longer. On Oct 11, 2010 it was confirmed by GRRM's editor Anne Groell that Martin has finished all but five chapters for A Dance with Dragons, and that the five chapters remaining already exist in partial form. She also teases the hope of the publisher that the manuscript will be finished by Christmas 2010.

Supplementary works

There are also three novellas based on chapter sets from the books:

- *Blood of the Dragon* is a novella taken from the Daenerys chapters in *A Game of Thrones*. It won the Hugo Award for Best Novella in 1997.
- *Path of the Dragon* is a second novella based on the Daenerys chapters, this time taken from *A Storm of Swords*.
- *Arms of the Kraken* is a novella based on the Iron Islands chapters from *A Feast for Crows*.

There are also three separate novellas set in the same world, known as the "Tales of Dunk and Egg" after the main protagonists. They are set about ninety years before the novels and for now have no direct connection with the plot of *A Song of Ice and Fire*.

- *The Hedge Knight* (1998)
- *The Sworn Sword* (2003)
- *The Mystery Knight* (2010)

The Hedge Knight and *The Sworn Sword* are also both available as graphic novels from Dabel Brothers Productions. The author has said that he would like to write a number of these stories (varying from six to twelve from interview to interview) covering the entire lives of these two characters. The third "Dunk and Egg" novella, titled *The Mystery Knight*, was published in March 2010 in the anthology *Warriors*, edited by Martin and Gardner Dozois.

A companion volume for the series is in development by George R. R. Martin and co-authors Elio M. García, Jr. and Linda Antonsson, although no publication date has been confirmed as yet. García and Antonsson run the largest *A Song of Ice and Fire* community on the web and assisted in the writing of the first roleplaying game. The companion volume was given the working title *The World of Ice and Fire* at the 2006 Worldcon during a discussion between the writers. They confirmed that the book will open with a historical overview of the setting, have a "who's who" of characters and have a large amount of heraldry and at least the Targaryen family tree, and possibly more. The book will contain a large amount of artwork and will be published after *A Dance with Dragons* is released. The artist Ted Nasmith, best known for his work on illustrated editions of J. R. R. Tolkien books, has been asked to do some landscape and castle portraits for the book. In his correspondence with the publishers, Nasmith was told that the target release date was spring 2008, although the book was subsequently moved back.

Reception

- *A Game of Thrones* (1996) - Locus Award **winner**, Nebula and World Fantasy Awards nominee, 1997
- *A Clash of Kings* (1998) - Locus Award **winner**, Nebula Award nominee, 1999
- *A Storm of Swords* (2000) - Locus Award **winner**, Hugo and Nebula Awards nominee, 2001
- *A Feast for Crows* (2005) - Hugo, Locus, and British Fantasy Awards nominee, 2006

Adaptation

Main article: Game of Thrones (TV series)

In March 2010, HBO greenlighted a television series based on *A Song of Ice and Fire*, with David Benioff and Dan Weiss attached to write and executive produce. Called *Game of Thrones*, it stars Sean Bean, Peter Dinklage, and Lena Headey. The series will cover one novel's worth of material per season, and is expected to debut in Spring 2011.

Franchise

Main articles: A Game of Thrones collectible card game, A Game of Thrones (board game), and A Game of Thrones (role-playing game)

A collectible card game (CCG) has been produced by Fantasy Flight Games. A number of base sets have been released for the game, each with a number of expansions. The game's primary designer is Eric Lang and the lead developer is Nate French. The *A Game of Thrones: Westeros Edition* won the Origins Award for *Best Trading Card Game of 2002*. The *Game of Thrones: Ice and Fire Edition* won the Origins Award for *Best Card Game Expansion or Supplement of 2003*. It is an ongoing project consisting of five editions and eight expansions to date.

In 2003, Fantasy Flight Games released the *A Game of Thrones* strategy board game created by Christian T. Petersen. The Origins Award-winning game allows the players to take on the roles of several of the Great Houses vying for control of the Seven Kingdoms, including House Stark, House Lannister, House Baratheon, House Greyjoy, House Tyrell, and as of the expansion *A Clash of Kings*, House Martell. Players maneuver armies to secure support in the various regions that comprise the Seven Kingdoms, with the goal of capturing enough support to claim the Iron Throne. Two expansions for the game, *A Clash of Kings* and *A Storm of Swords* have been released.

The *A Game of Thrones Roleplaying Game* (2005), created by the defunct Guardians of Order company and published by White Wolf, is a roleplaying game using the d20 and the Tri-Stat dX rules systems. The game consists of a single large, full-colour rulebook featuring information on role-playing in the Seven Kingdoms and also background information to the series not found in the novels, including a detailed map of the Seven Kingdoms. The game was very well-received and was nominated for several awards (and won 3 silver ENnie awards for Best Production, Best Game, and Best d20/OGL Product), but this was not enough to save its parent company from closure in July 2006.

On 28 July 2006 George R. R. Martin confirmed [1] that he had received word from the head of Guardians of Order that the company was folding and that no further releases for the setting would take place. Martin expressed hope that the game might be salvaged by another company, and on 24 April 2007, Green Ronin Publishing announced [2] they would be producing a new role-playing game titled *A Song of Ice and Fire.*

Green Ronin has or will publish the following titles:

- "A Song of Ice and Fire Roleplaying Quick-Start Rules" (free PDF) (June 21, 2008)
- "A Song of Ice and Fire Roleplaying: Adventures in the Seven Kingdoms" (rulebook) (ISBN 978-1-934547-12-0, 10 March 2009)
- "A Song of Ice and Fire Narrator's Kit" (ISBN 978-1-934547-28-1, 21 May 2009)
- "Peril at King's Landing" (adventure) (ISBN 978-1-934547-16-8, 13 August 2009)
- "A Song of Ice and Fire Campaign Guide" (ISBN 978-1-934547-13-7, 18 February 2010)
- "A Song of Ice and Fire Roleplaying: Pocket Edition" (ISBN 978-1-934547-34-2, no release date announced)

Blood of Dragons is an online, text-based roleplaying MUSH and the only online game specifically authorized by the author as of February 2009. *Blood of Dragons* fully opened in 2007 and is set approximately 140 years prior to the initial series, during the reign of Daeron I and his conquest of Dorne. The game is maintained by the administrators of Westeros.org, who are collaborating with Martin on *The World of Ice and Fire.*

On May 13, 2009 Cyanide Studio announced they will be developing a series of video games based on *A Song of Ice and Fire* for the PC and consoles.. Martin has since revealed that both an RTS and an RPG game are currently in development.

The Art of Ice and Fire, published in 2005 by Fantasy Flight Games, contains numerous works of art inspired by the series from a variety of different artists and illustrators. Some of the art previously appeared in the card game or on-line, but most of it was new.

Testor Corporation announced that in late 2006 it would begin releasing model figures based on the series, to be followed by a tactical wargame. Only one product shipped, a Ruby Ford diorama. In April 2007, Martin announced that the licensing agreement with Testor had expired, and Testor's *A Song of Ice and Fire* product lines had been canceled. In December 2006, Haute Productions signed a deal to release a range of resin mini-busts featuring characters from *A Song of Ice and Fire*, under the name Valyrian Resin. The company plans to expand the line to include resin statues and pewter chess sets. On August 13, 2007, Dark Sword Miniatures announced a line of premium pewter miniatures based on the world of George R. R. Martin's *A Song of Ice and Fire*, and sculpted by renowned miniatures artist Tom Meier.

On 20 March 2007, George R. R. Martin announced on his blog that he had "signed a deal with Jalic, Inc of East Lansing, Michigan, granting them a license to manufacture and sell full-sized high-quality replicas of the arms and armor from *A Song of Ice and Fire*", under the name Valyrian Steel, starting with the bastard sword Longclaw wielded by Jon Snow. As of early 2009, Jalic has had Arya Stark's Needle from “A Song of Ice and Fire” on pre-sale. Both Needle and Longclaw are currently listed and available in a Limited Edition of 2500 each.

The German power metal band Blind Guardian have written two songs dedicated to the world of George R. R. Martin's *A Song of Ice and Fire*. The songs are called "War of the Thrones" and "A Voice in the Dark" and are part of their 2010 At the Edge of Time album .

External links

- George R. R. Martin's Official Website [3]
- A Song of Ice and Fire [4] at the Open Directory Project
- So Spake Martin [5] – extensive archive of correspondence from the author to the fans

The Author

George R. R. Martin

George R. R. Martin	

George R. R. Martin (2007)	
Born	September 20, 1948 Bayonne, New Jersey
Occupation	Author
Genres	Science fiction, Horror, Fantasy
Notable work(s)	*A Song of Ice and Fire*
[1]	

George Raymond Richard Martin (born September 20, 1948), sometimes referred to as **GRRM**, is an American author and screenwriter of fantasy, horror, and science fiction. He is best known for his ongoing *A Song of Ice and Fire* series of epic fantasy novels.

Biography

George R. R. Martin was born on September 20, 1948 in Bayonne, New Jersey. As a youth, Martin became an avid reader and collector of comic books. *Fantastic Four* #20 (Nov 1963) features a letter to the editor he wrote while in high school. He credits the attention he received from this letter, as well as his following interest in comics fanzines, with his interest in becoming a writer.

Martin wrote short fiction in the early 1970s and while his start into the professional writer career was not easy (one of his stories was rejected by different magazines forty-two times) he was not discouraged and later won several Hugo Awards and Nebula Awards. His first story to be nominated for Hugo and Nebula Award was *With Morning Comes Mistfall* published by the Analog magazine in 1973. The story lost both Awards, but Martin didn't mind too much, noting that joining "Hugo-and-Nebula Losers" Club was a big enough accomplishment for him.

In 1976 at Kansas City's MidAmeriCon, the 34th World Science Fiction Convention, Martin, with old friend Gardner Dozois, conceived of and organized the first ever Hugo Losers Party, a gathering spot for the losers (and their friends and family), immediately following KC's Hugo Awards ceremony. The party had been planned well in advance, and in a strong note of irony, Martin lost again in 1976, but this time it was for *two* Hugo Awards: the Novelette "...and Seven Times Never Kill Man" and the Novella "The Storms of Windhaven," co-written with Lisa Tuttle. In the years and decades that followed, the Hugo Losers Party has become an annual event, evolving into one of the largest social gatherings held at the annual Worldcon.

Although much of his work is fantasy or horror, a number of his earlier works are science fiction occurring in a loosely-defined future history, known informally as 'The Thousand Worlds' or 'The manrealm'. He has also written at least one piece of political-military fiction, "Night of the Vampyres", collected in Harry Turtledove's anthology *The Best Military Science Fiction of the 20th Century*.

In the 1980s he turned to work in television and as a book editor. On television, he worked on the new *Twilight Zone* and *Beauty and the Beast* series. As an editor, he oversaw the lengthy *Wild Cards* cycle, which took place in a shared universe in which an alien virus bestowed strange powers or disfigurements on a slice of humanity during World War II, affecting the history of the world thereafter (the premise was inspired by comic book superheroes and a Superworld superhero role-playing game of which Martin was gamemaster). Contributors to the *Wild Cards* series included Stephen Leigh, Lewis Shiner, Howard Waldrop, Walter Jon Williams and Roger Zelazny. His own contributions to the series often featured Thomas Tudbury, "The Great and Powerful Turtle", a powerful psychokinetic whose flying "shell" consisted of an armored VW Beetle.

Martin's novella, *Nightflyers*, was adapted into a 1987 feature film.

In 1991 Martin briefly returned to writing novel-length stories, and began what would eventually turn into his epic fantasy series, *A Song of Ice and Fire* (ostensibly inspired by the Wars of the Roses and Ivanhoe), which is projected to run to seven volumes. The first volume *A Game of Thrones* was published in 1996. In November 2005, *A Feast for Crows*, the fourth book in this series, became *The New York Times* #1 Bestseller and also achieved #1 ranking on *The Wall Street Journal* bestseller list. In addition, in September 2006 *A Feast for Crows* was nominated for both a Quill award, and the British Fantasy Award. The series has received praise from authors, readers and critics alike.

HBO Productions purchased the television rights for the entire *A Song of Ice and Fire* series in 2007, and greenlit the first season in March 2010, for a predicted 2011 premiere. The first season will be based on the first novel in the series.

In 2008, Fantasy Flight Games released the boardgame "The Game Of Thrones" and in 2010 "The Battles of Westeros," a miniatures boardgame based on the battles depicted in the "A Song of Fire and Ice" series.

Martin has also been an instructor in journalism (in which he holds a master's degree) and a chess tournament director. In his spare time he collects medieval-themed miniatures and continues to treasure his comic collection, which includes the first issues of *Spider-Man* and *Fantastic Four*. Although he is fairly active on the internet, he notes: "I do my writing on a completely different computer than the one I use for email and the internet, in part to guard against viruses, worms, and nightmares like this. (...) I write with WordStar 4.0 on a pure DOS-based machine."

Themes

George R. R. Martin, circa 1986

Critics have described Martin's work as dark and cynical. His first novel, *Dying of the Light*, set the tone for most of his future work; it is set on a mostly abandoned planet that is slowly becoming uninhabitable as it moves away from its sun. This story, and many of Martin's others, have a strong sense of melancholy. His characters are often unhappy, or at least unsatisfied - trying to stay idealistic in a ruthless world. Many have elements of tragic heroes in them. Reviewer T. M. Wagner writes, "Let it never be said Martin doesn't share Shakespeare's fondness for the senselessly tragic." This gloominess can be an obstacle for some readers. The Inchoatus Group writes, "If this absence of joy is going to trouble you, or you're looking for something more affirming, then you should probably seek elsewhere."

Martin's characters are multi-faceted, each with surprisingly intricate pasts, inspirations, and ambitions. *Publisher's Weekly* writes of his on-going epic fantasy *A Song of Ice and Fire* "The complexity of characters such as Daenarys [sic], Arya and the Kingslayer will keep readers turning even the vast number of pages contained in this volume, for the author, like Tolkien or Jordan, makes us care about their fates." No one is given an unrealistic string of luck, however, so misfortune, injury, and death (and even false death) can befall *any* character, major or minor, no matter how attached the reader has become. Martin has described his penchant for killing off important characters as being necessary for the story's depth: "...when my characters are in danger, I want you to be afraid to turn the page, (so) you need to show right from the beginning that you're playing for keeps."

His novels and short-stories often have a religious background and question the reader about religion, either overtly, dealing about one existing or imaginary religion, or instilled with religious questionnement; this last feature appears for example in Tuf Voyaging , in which the ability of human being to assume a godly role is underlying. Similarly, *A Song of Ice and Fire* contains many instances where the characters try to communicate with gods, yet receiving no answers in return.

Fan relationship

In addition to writing, Martin is known for his regular attendance at science fiction conventions and his accessibility to fans. In the early 70s, critic and writer Thomas Disch identified Martin as a member of the "Labor Day Group", writers who congregated at the annual Worldcon, usually held around Labor Day.

Teaching at Clarion West, 1998.

Martin has a good relationship with his official fan club, the Brotherhood Without Banners, and has praised them in the past for their parties and philanthropic efforts. As of December 2006, the organization has more than 1,000 official members listed on its website.

Martin has been criticized by many fans for the long delay between books in the *A Song of Ice and Fire* series, most recently the many-year gap before the next volume, *A Dance with Dragons*, which has led the author to respond, accusing angry fans of unfairly demanding he devote all his time to the series.

Martin is very strongly opposed to fan fiction, believing it to be copyright infringement and bad exercise for aspiring writers. He does not give permission for any of his intellectual property to be used in fan fiction.

Bibliography

Author

Novels

- *Dying of the Light* (1977) -- Hugo Award nominee, 1978 ; British Fantasy Award nominee, 1979
- *Windhaven* (1981, with Lisa Tuttle) -- Locus SF Award nominee, 1982
- *Fevre Dream* (1982) -- Locus SF and World Fantasy Award nominee, 1983
- *The Armageddon Rag* (1983) -- Locus SF and World Fantasy Award nominee, 1984
- *A Song of Ice and Fire* series:
  - *A Game of Thrones* (1996) -- Locus Fantasy Award Winner, Nebula and World Fantasy Award nominee, 1997
  - *A Clash of Kings* (1998) -- Nebula Award nominee, 1999; Locus Fantasy Award winner, 1999
  - *A Storm of Swords* (2000) -- Locus Fantasy Award winner, Hugo and Nebula Awards nominee, 2001
  - *A Feast for Crows* (2005) -- Hugo, Locus Fantasy, and British Fantasy Awards nominee, 2006
  - *A Dance with Dragons* (forthcoming)
  - *The Winds of Winter* (forthcoming)
  - *A Dream of Spring* (forthcoming)
- *Hunter's Run* (2007, expanded version of the novella "Shadow Twin", with Gardner Dozois and Daniel Abraham)

Martin announced on the 8th of July 2010 that he was '1,400' pages into finishing A Dance with Dragons.

Selected novellas

- "A Song for Lya", originally in *Analog*, June 1974.
- Night of the Vampyres, originally in *Amazing*, 1975 [2], re-published in *The Best Military Science Fiction of the 20th Century*
- "The Skin Trade" (1989) from the three-author collection Dark Visions.

The werewolf novella "The Skin Trade," has been optioned for film by Mike the Pike Productions.

- "Tales of Dunk and Egg" series - set in the world of *A Song of Ice and Fire*
  - "The Hedge Knight" (1998)
  - "The Sworn Sword" (2003)
  - "The Mystery Knight" (2010)
- "Shadow Twin" (2004, with Gardner Dozois and Daniel Abraham)

Selected novelettes

- *Sandkings*, Martins most anthologized story to date and the only one of his to win both the Hugo *and* the Nebula awards.
- *Meathouse Man*, first published in 1976, in *Orbit* 18. (Originally intended for Harlan Ellison's notorious *"The Last Dangerous Visions"* anthology, GRRM has admitted that this is probably the darkest, most depressing story he has ever done and that he still finds it painful to re-read nearly thirty years after its publication.)

Children's books

- *The Ice Dragon* (Originally printed in 1980 as a short story, illustrated and re-printed as a children's book in October, 2006)

Collections

- *A Song for Lya* (1976)
- *Songs of Stars and Shadows* (1977)
- *Sandkings* (1981)
- *Songs the Dead Men Sing* (1983)
- *Nightflyers* (1985)
- *Tuf Voyaging* (1987, collection of linked stories)
- *Portraits of His Children* (1987)
- *Quartet* (2001)
- *GRRM: A RRetrospective* (2003; reissued 2006 and 2007 as *Dreamsongs*)

Television

- *The Twilight Zone*
  - *The Last Defender of Camelot* (1986) - writer (teleplay)
  - *The Once and Future King* (1986) - writer (teleplay), story editor
  - *A Saucer of Loneliness* (1986) - story editor
  - *Lost and Found* (1986) - writer (teleplay), from a printed short story by Phyllis Eisenstein
  - *The World Next Door* (1986) - story editor
  - *The Toys of Caliban* (1986) - writer (teleplay), from an unpublshed short story by Terry Matz
  - *The Road Less Travelled* (1986) - writer (story and teleplay), story editor
- *Beauty and the Beast*
  - *Terrible Saviour* (1987) - writer
  - *Masques* (1987) - writer
  - *Shades of Grey* (1988) - writer
  - *Promises of Someday* (1988) - writer

  - *Fever* (1988) - writer
  - *Ozymandias* (1988) - writer
  - *Dead of Winter* (1988) - writer
  - *Brothers* (1989) - writer
  - *When the Blue Bird Sings' (1989) - writer (teleplay)*
  - *A Kingdom by the Sea* (1989) - writer
  - *What Rough Beast* (1989) - writer (story)
  - *Ceremony of Innocence* (1989) - writer
  - *Snow* (1989) - writer
  - *Beggar's Comet* (1990) - writer
  - *Invictus* (1990) - writer
- *Doorways* (1993, unreleased pilot) - writer, producer, creator (*IDW Publishing* is publishing the pilot as a graphic novel miniseries (2010))
- *A Game of Thrones*
  - Pilot (in pre-production) - writer (story, teleplay), producer, creator

Editor

Wild Cards (also contributor to many volumes)

- *Wild Cards I* (1987)
- *Wild Cards II: Aces High* (1987)
- *Wild Cards III: Jokers Wild* (1987)
- *Wild Cards IV: Aces Abroad* (1988)
- *Wild Cards V: Down & Dirty* (1988)
- *Wild Cards VI: Ace in the Hole* (1990)
- *Wild Cards VII: Dead Man's Hand* (1990)
- *Wild Cards VIII: One-Eyed Jacks* (1991)
- *Wild Cards IX: Jokertown Shuffle* (1991)
- *Wild Cards X: Double Solitaire* (1992)
- *Wild Cards XI: Dealer's Choice* (1992)
- *Wild Cards XII: Turn of the Cards* (1993)

- *Wild Cards: Card Sharks* (1993) (Book I of a New Cycle trilogy)
- *Wild Cards: Marked Cards* (1994) (Book II of a New Cycle trilogy)
- *Wild Cards: Black Trump* (1995) (Book III of a New Cycle trilogy)

- *Wild Cards: Deuces Down* (2002)
- *Wild Cards: Death Draws Five* (2006)
- *Wild Cards: Inside Straight* (2008) (Book I of the Committee triad)

- *Wild Cards: Busted Flush* (2008) (Book II of the Committee triad)
- *Wild Cards: Suicide Kings* (2009) (Book III of the Committee triad)
- *Wild Cards: Fort Freak* (delivered) (A stand-alone novel)

Cross-genre anthologies edited (with Gardner Dozois)

- *Warriors* a massive, cross-genre anthology featuring stories about war and warriors (published on March 16, 2010)
- *Songs of the Dying Earth* a tribute anthology to Jack Vance´s seminal Dying Earth series, initially published by Subterranean Press (2009)
- *Songs of Love and Death* a cross-genre anthology featuring stories of romance in fantasy and science-fiction settings (originally entitled *Star Crossed Lovers*; November, 2010)
- *Down These Strange Streets* another cross-genre anthology, blending classic private eye detective stories with fantasy and science fiction (forthcoming)

Awards

- "A Song for Lya" 1975 Hugo Award for Best Novella
- "Sandkings" 1980 Hugo Award for Best Novelette and Nebula Award for Best Novelette (the only one among Martin's stories to achieve that double)
- "The Way of Cross and Dragon" 1980 Hugo Award for Best Short Story
- "Portraits of His Children" 1986 Nebula Award for Best Novelette
- "The Pear-Shaped Man" 1988 Bram Stoker Award for Long Fiction
- "The Skin Trade" 1989 World Fantasy Award for Best Novella
- "Blood of the Dragon" 1997 Hugo Award for Best Novella
- "A Feast for Crows" 2006 Quill award and British Fantasy Award (nominated)

A more complete list of Martin's awards and nominations [3] can be found at The *Locus* Index to Science Fiction Awards.

External links

- George R. R. Martin official site [1]
- Not A Blog: George R. R. Martin's Livejournal [4]
- George R. R. Martin's Podcast [5]
- George R. R. Martin Complete Bibliography [6]
- George R.R. Martin [7] at the Internet Book List
- George R. R. Martin [8] at the Internet Speculative Fiction Database
- Brotherhood without Banners [9] - official fan club

Interviews

- 2010 Interview on the Geek's Guide to the Galaxy Podcast [10]
- Interview with George R.R. Martin at Neth Space [11]
- Interview with George R.R. Martin [12] at SFFWorld.com
- Interview with George R. R. Martin in Abebooks.com [13]
- Audio interview with National Review Online [14]
- Audio Interview with George R.R. Martin [15] at Geekson.com
- Interview with fiction writer George R.R. Martin [16] at FreeMagazine.fi
- In a Fantasy World of His Own [17] Northwestern magazine profile

The Books

A Game of Thrones

A Game of Thrones	
US Hardcover (2002 Bantam Reissue)	
Author	George R. R. Martin
Cover artist	Steve Youll
Country	United States
Language	English
Series	A Song of Ice and Fire
Genre(s)	Fantasy
Publisher	Bantam Spectra (US) & Voyager Books (UK)
Publication date	6 August 1996
Media type	Print (Hardback & Paperback)
Pages	694 pp (US Hardback), 672 pp (UK Hardcover), 835 pp (US Paperback)
ISBN	ISBN 0-553-10354-7 (US Hardback), ISBN 0-00-224584-1 (UK Hardback), ISBN 0-553-57340-3 (US Paperback)
OCLC Number	33360758 [1]
Dewey Decimal	813/.54 20
LC Classification	PS3563.A7239 G36 1996
Followed by	*A Clash of Kings*

A Game of Thrones is the first of seven planned novels in ***A Song of Ice and Fire***, an epic fantasy series by American author George R. R. Martin. It was first published on 6 August 1996. The novel won the 1997 Locus Award, and was nominated for both the 1998 Nebula Award and the 1997 World Fantasy Award. The novella *Blood of the Dragon*, comprising the Daenerys Targaryen chapters from the novel, won the 1997 Hugo Award for Best Novella.

The novel lends its name to several spin-off items based on the novels, including a trading card game, board game, and roleplaying game. In November 2009 HBO completed filming of a pilot episode for the television adaptation.

Plot summary

A Game of Thrones follows three principal storylines simultaneously.

In the Seven Kingdoms

At Winterfell, northern seat of Lord Eddard Stark. his bastard son Jon finds a dead direwolf with six pups. As the direwolf is the symbol of House Stark, Eddard allows each of his children to keep one as pet, including the bastard son.

King Robert Baratheon arrives in Winterfell with his entourage to ask Eddard to become Hand of the King, as the previous hand, Lord Jon Arryn, has died recently. Eddard reluctantly agrees and travels south with his daughters Sansa and Arya

During the visit, Eddard's wife, Catelyn Stark, receives a letter from her sister Lysa Arryn, stating that Jon Arryn was murdered by House Lannister; Eddard's middle son Bran Stark accidentally sees Cersei and her twin brother Jaime being intimate, and Jaime throws him out of a tower window. Bran survives, yet is crippled, losing the use of his legs; Jon Snow leaves Winterfell to join the Night's Watch in the far North.

An assassination attempt with an unusual dagger is made on Bran, so Catelyn travels to the capital King's Landing to tell her husband of the attack. Her friend Petyr Baelish identifies the dagger as belonging to Tyrion Lannister. On her way home she meets Tyrion on the road and orders him taken captive to the Eyrie, where her sister Lysa places him on trial. Tyrion demands trial by combat and regains his freedom when his champion wins the fight.

At King's Landing, Eddard investigates Jon Arryn's death and learns that Jon and King Robert's brother Lord Stannis Baratheon had discovered that Robert's and Queen Cersei's three children were actually fathered by her twin brother Jaime. Eddard mercifully offers Cersei the chance to flee, but she refuses. King Robert dies while hunting, (under suspicious conditions) and Cersei's eldest son Joffrey is crowned King, although Stannis is Robert's true heir, as he is his elder brother. Eddard is betrayed by Littlefinger and the Lannisters and captured. Eddard reluctantly agrees to a false confession of treason in return for his daughters' lives, and the chance to go into exile on the Wall. But Joffrey has Eddard brutally executed in public. While Sansa is retained in custody, Arya escapes during the sack of King's Landing, and witnesses her father's execution while living in Flea Bottom. A civil war, later dubbed the War of the Five Kings, erupts. On the pretext of seeking retribution for the capture of his son Tyrion, Lord Tywin Lannister attacks Riverrun, the Tully stronghold. Robb Stark leads an army of northmen into the Riverlands to support Lord Hoster Tully, seek revenge for the death of his father and secure the

North as an independent realm. Jaime Lannister leads the siege, while Lord Tywin holds a large army south of the River Trident to prevent Robb's advance. Robb and Catelyn win House Frey's support by agreeing to a dynastic marriage, among numerous other concessions. Robb detaches his cavalry and crosses the Green Fork while his infantry carries on to the Trident under Lord Roose Bolton, one of Robb's bannermen. Tywin, joined by the liberated Tyrion (who has won the support of the mountain clans of the Vale), defeats the Stark footmen before learning that Robb has outmaneuvered him. Shortly afterwards Robb's forces surprise and capture Jaime at the Battle of Whispering Wood and destroy the rest of the Lannister army besieging Riverrun. Tywin falls back to Harrenhal and orders Tyrion, whose cunning and intelligence he has come to reluctantly respect, to go to King's Landing to serve as Hand of the King in Tywin's absence.

Lord Renly Baratheon declares himself King of Westeros, becoming the second of the war's five kings. Robb Stark becomes the third when all Stark and Tully bannermen proclaim him the King in the North and the Riverlands.

On the Wall

Men of the Night's Watch range on a mission beyond the Wall. They come across a camp of wildings seemingly frozen to death. They encounter the fabled 'Others' of legend, and are killed except for one man who flees south, where Eddard executes him as a deserter.

Jon Snow, seeing little future for himself as the bastard son of Eddard, chooses to join the Night's Watch. He travels north with his uncle Benjen Stark, the First Ranger of the Watch. At the Wall Jon finds that the Watch is beset with problems. A new King-beyond-the-Wall, Mance Rayder, has arisen in the northern lands. The Watch is grievously under strength, and its manpower is now made up of criminals who chose the Wall over execution or imprisonment.

Jon befriends the other new recruits and Samwell Tarly, a timid but intelligent boy, and Maester Aemon. Aemon is a Targaryen, great uncle to the deposed Mad King Aerys II.

Jon earns the status of full brother of the Night's Watch. To his dismay, he is assigned as a steward to Jeor Mormont, the Lord Commander of the Watch. Sam points out that Mormont is grooming Jon for command. The Watch bring two corpses back from beyond the Wall, but they re-animate as wights that night. One attacks the Commander's Tower, including Mormont, while the second confronts the men of the Night's Watch. Jon destroys the one attacking Mormont with fire, destroying Mormont's quarters as well, while the other slays two men and then is hacked into to pieces by a dozen Night's Watch soldiers. Mormont gives Jon his Valyrian-steel bastard sword, Longclaw, as thanks for saving him from the walking corpse.

In the East

Across the sea in the Free City of Pentos, the exiled Prince Viserys Targaryen conspires to sell his thirteen-year-old sister Daenerys to Khal Drogo of the Dothraki. Viserys plans to use Drogo's army to reclaim the kingship of Westeros. Among the wedding gifts are three petrified dragon eggs. Unexpectedly, Daenerys finds trust and love with Drogo, and she conceives a child. Ser Jorah Mormont, a knight exiled from Westeros for dealing in slaves, joins Viserys as an advisor.

Khal Drogo sees his marriage to Daenerys as advantageous, but has little interest in conquering Westeros. Viserys, humiliated and angry, begins to provoke his hosts. They endure it for a while; eventually Drogo kills him for threatening Daenerys. She takes up her brother's quest to reclaim the Iron Throne. When a Westerosi assassin tries to kill her and their unborn child, Drogo agrees to invade Westeros. However, an unrelated skirmish soon after leads to his death of infection, and Daenerys loses her unborn son to the machinations of a shamaness. Danaerys orders her tied to Khal Drogo's funerals pyre and then walks into the flames with the three dragon eggs. Miraculously, she is unscathed by the raging flames and the dragon eggs hatch in the heat.

Viewpoint characters

Each chapter concentrates on one character in a third person limited point of view. Each chapter bears the name of the current POV character (ex. "Bran," "Catelyn," "Daenerys") with the story flipping back and forth between the main characters.

The tale of *A Game of Thrones* is told through the eyes of 8 POV characters and a one-off prologue POV.

- Prologue: Will, a man of the Night's Watch.
- Lord Eddard Stark, Warden of the North and Lord of Winterfell, Hand of the King.
- Lady Catelyn Stark, of House Tully, wife of Eddard Stark.
- Sansa Stark, elder daughter of Eddard and Catelyn Stark.
- Arya Stark, younger daughter of Eddard and Catelyn Stark.
- Bran Stark, middle of three sons of Eddard and Catelyn Stark.
- Jon Snow, bastard son of Eddard Stark.
- Tyrion Lannister, a dwarf,Queen Cersei's brother and son of Lord Tywin Lannister.
- Princess Daenerys Targaryen, Stormborn, the Princess of Dragonstone and heiress to the Targaryen throne after her older brother Viserys Targaryen.

Editions

In June 2000 Meisha Merlin released a limited edition of the book, fully illustrated by Jeffrey Jones.

Foreign language editions

- Bulgarian: "*Игра на тронове*"
- Catalan: Devir Contenidos (2006): *"La mà del rei"*
- Chinese: 重庆出版社(2005): *"权力的游戏"*.
- Croatian: *"Igra prijestolja"*
- Czech: *"Hra o trůny"*
- Dutch: Luitingh-Sijthoff (1997): *"Het spel der tronen"*
- Estonian: Two volumes, Varrak (2006): *"Troonide mäng"*
- Finnish: *"Valtaistuinpeli"* (2003)
- French: Two volumes (hardcover: Pygmalion (1998, 1999); paperback: J'ai Lu (2001)) *"Le trône de fer"*, *"Le donjon rouge"*.
- German: Single volume, Fantasy Productions (2004): *"Eisenthron"*. Two volumes, Goldmann (1997, 1998): *"Die Herren von Winterfell"*, *"Das Erbe von Winterfell"*
- Greek: Two volumes, Anubis (2004): *"Παιχνίδι του στέμματος"*
- Hebrew: משחקי הכס
- Hungarian: Single volume, Alexandra: *"Trónok harca"*
- Italian: Two volumes, Mondadori (hardcover: 1999, 2000; paperback: 2001): *"Il trono di spade"*, *"Il grande inverno"*; as a single volume titled *"Il gioco del trono"* in the collection *Urania Fantasy - Le grandi saghe* (July 2007)
- Japanese: *"七王国の玉座"* (The Seven Kingdom's Throne) Hayakawa Publishing Corporation 2002 Hardcover, 2 volumes; 2006 Softcover, 5 volumes.
- Korean: "왕좌의 게임"
- Polish: Zysk (1998): *"Gra o tron"*
- Portuguese: Two volumes: Saída de Emergência (2007): *"A Guerra dos Tronos"*, *"A Muralha de Gelo"*. Partial and pirate edition: Entre Letras Editora (2002): *"A Muralha"* (1st part only)
- Romanian: : Two volumes: *"Urzeala tronurilor"* (2007)
- Russian: Single volume, AST (2001, 2004, 2007): *"Игра престолов"*. Two volumes, AST (1999): *"Игра престолов. Книга 1"*, *"Игра престолов. Книга 2"*.
- Serbian: Laguna (2003): *"Igra Prestola"*
- Slovene: *"Igra prestolov"* (2007)
- Spanish: Gigamesh (2002): *"Juego de tronos"*
- Swedish: Two volumes, Forum: *"I vargens tid"*, *"Kampen om järntronen"*. Single volume, Forum (2005): *"Kampen om järntronen"*
- Turkish: Buz ve Ateşin Şarkısı Serisi: *"Taht Oyunları"* (2005)

TV Show

Game of Thrones (TV series) will be made into an HBO series premiering in 2011.

Literary significance and criticism

- Pelletier, J. K. "FantasyBookNews.com" [2].
- Wagner, T. M.. "SF Reviews.Net" [3].
- Seidman, James. "SF Site" [4].
- Silver, Steven H.. "SFF World" [5].

Awards and nominations

- Locus Award – Best Novel (Fantasy) (Won) – (1997)
- World Fantasy Award – Best Novel (Nominated) – (1997)
- Hugo Award – Best Novella for *Blood of the Dragon* (Won) – (1997)
- Nebula Award – Best Novel (Nominated) – (1997)
- Ignotus Award – Best Novel (Foreign) (Won) – (2003)

External links

- George R.R. Martin's 'Game Of Thrones' Greenlit By HBO [6]

A Clash of Kings

A Clash of Kings	
US Hardcover Edition	
Author	George R. R. Martin
Cover artist	Steve Youll
Country	United States
Language	English
Series	A Song of Ice and Fire
Genre(s)	Fantasy
Publisher	Bantam Spectra (US) & Voyager Books (UK)
Publication date	November 1998 (UK) & March 1999 (US)
Media type	Print (Hardback & Paperback)
Pages	708 (UK Hardback), 768 (US Hardback), 1009 (US Paperback)
ISBN	ISBN 0-00-224585-X (UK Hardback), ISBN 0-553-10803-4 (US Hardback), ISBN 0-553-57990-8 (US Paperback)
OCLC Number	59667381 [1]
Preceded by	*A Game of Thrones*
Followed by	*A Storm of Swords*

A Clash of Kings is the second of seven planned novels in ***A Song of Ice and Fire***, an epic fantasy series by American author George R. R. Martin. It was first published on 16 November 1998 in the United Kingdom, although the first United States edition did not follow until March 1999. Like its predecessor, *A Game of Thrones*, it won both the Locus Award (in 1999) for Best Novel and was nominated for the Nebula Award (also in 1999) for best novel.

In May 2005 Meisha Merlin released a much-delayed limited edition of the novel, fully illustrated by John Howe.

A Clash of Kings is also the name of the first expansion to the *A Game of Thrones* board game.

Plot introduction

The series is set in a fictitious world reminiscent of Medieval Europe, primarily on a continent called Westeros. In this world the seasons can last for years at a time, sometimes decades.

Plot summary

A Clash of Kings picks up where *A Game of Thrones* ended. The Seven Kingdoms of Westeros are plagued by civil war, while the Night's Watch mounts a reconnaissance force north of the Wall to investigate the mysterious people, known as wildlings, who live there. Meanwhile, in the distant east, Daenerys Targaryen continues her quest to return to and conquer the Seven Kingdoms. All signs are foreshadowing the terrible disaster that is to come.

In the Seven Kingdoms

The civil war to claim the Iron Throne becomes more complex, Greyjoys launches a massive assault along the west coast of The North. At the Stark stronghold Winterfell, Robb's young brother Bran Stark is in command; he finds two new friends when Jojen and Meera Reed arrive from Greywater Watch. They take an interest in his strange dreams.

Robert's brother Stannis Baratheon declares himself King of Westeros, encouraged by Melisandre, a red pristess of R'hllor. His younger brother Renly also claims the throne. Catelyn Stark joins a parley between Renly and Stannis to discuss a possible Stark-Baratheon alliance against their mutual foe, the Lannisters. The parley fails, and a strange shadow kills Renly in his tent. Catelyn flees along with the only other witness to this murder, the warrior-maid Brienne of Tarth. Most of Renly's supporters shift their loyalty to Stannis, but the Tyrells do not, and their stronghold Storm's End falls when Melisandre magically gives birth to another shadow to kill the castle's defiant castellan.

Tyrion Lannister arrives at King's Landing to become Hand of the King, the closest adviser to the monarch. Whilst intriguing against his sister Cersei, widow of the late king and mother of King Joffrey, Tyrion improves the defenses of the city and sends the devious Littlefinger to negotiate with the Tyrells. Lord Mace Tyrell agrees to wed his daughter Margaery to Joffrey. Additionaly, Joffrey's sister Princess Myrcella will wed Trystane Martell.

Theon Greyjoy, former ward of the Starks, captures Winterfell using just 20 men, taking Bran and Rickon Stark captive. Theon hopes to use Winterfell as a base to conquer the North. Bran and Rickon disappear in the night. Theon and his men pursue them without success, and he murders two peasant children to pass them off as the Stark princes. Stark supporters besiege the castle joined by a force from House Bolton, but the Bolton soldiers turn on them as planned. Theon opens the gates to the victorious Boltons but they raze Winterfell. Bran and Rickon emerge from hiding. and take separate courses: Osha, a captured wildling turned castle servant, agrees to take Rickon to safety, while Bran, accompanied by Meera and Jojen, decides to travel north to the Wall.

Robb Stark leads his army into the Westerlands and wins several victories against the Lannisters in their home territory. Tywin Lannister advances against him, but receiving news that King's Landing is threatened, rapidly withdraws south.

Arya Stark, posing as a boy named Arry to protect her identity as a wanted daughter of Stark, travels north along with new recruits for the Night's Watch. The group is captured and taken to Lannister-held Harrenhal, where Arya now poses as a peasant serving girl. A mysterious man, Jaqen H'ghar, repays Arya for saving his life by killing two men of her choice. Instead of choosing a third man, Arya cunningly enlists Jaquen's help to release a band of Stark supporters who quickly take over Harrenhal. Jaquen gives Arya a coin and a strange phrase "Valar Morghulis" to be used in a emergency. Lord Roose Bolton soon arrives to occupy Harrenhal. Arya becomes his page, but soon escapes.

Stannis Baratheon's army reaches King's Landing, An assault is launched by both land and sea. Under Tyrion's command, this force is thrown back by cunning use of "wildfire", a Greek Fire-like substance, to set fire to the river and by raising a chain across it to prevent Stannis' fleet from retreating essentially trapping them in the fiery bay. Stannis barely manages to escape with a decimated army and a few ships. Tyrion is seriously injured during the battle as a result of a treacherous attack.

On the Wall

A scouting party from the Night's Watch advances northwards from the Wall. At Craster's Keep they learn that the normally anarchic wildlings are uniting under a single figure, King-beyond-the-Wall Mance Rayder. The Watch continues north to a ruined fortress formerly known as the Fist of the First Men. Lord Commander Jeor Mormont sends Jon Snow and Qhorin Halfhand on an advanced reconnaissance of the Skirling Pass.

In the pass, Snow and Halfhand find themselves being hunted by several wildling warriors. Facing certain defeat, Halfhand commands Snow to act as an oathbreaker to infiltrate the wildlings and learn their plans. As proof he has truly turned, the wildlings force Jon to fight Halfhand, whom he kills with the aid of his direwolf Ghost. Jon learns that Rayder is already advancing on the Wall with tens of thousands of fighters.

In the East

Daenerys Targaryen strikes east across the forbidding red waste, accompanied by the knight Jorah Mormont, her remaining few loyal followers, and three newborn dragons. Scouts find a safe route to the great trading city of Qarth. Daenerys is the wonder of the city for her dragons, but cannot secure commitment from the merchants for claiming the throne of Westeros. In the House of the Undying, the powerful warlocks of Qarth show Daenerys many confusing images and her life is threatened. Daenerys' dragon Drogon burns down the House of the Undying, sparking the enmity of the Qartheen. An attempt to assassinate Daenerys at the city's harbor is thwarted by the arrival of two strangers, a fat warrior named Strong Belwas and his squire, an aged warrior named Arstan Whitebeard. They are agents of Daenerys's ally Illyrio Mopatis, come to escort her back to Pentos. Daenerys and her followers leave the city.

Characters

The tale is told through the eyes of 9 POV characters and a one-off prologue POV:

- Prologue: Maester Cressen, maester at Dragonstone.
- Tyrion Lannister, youngest son of Lord Tywin Lannister, a dwarf and a brother to Queen Cersei
- Lady Catelyn Stark, of House Tully, widow of Eddard Stark, Lord of Winterfell
- Ser Davos Seaworth, a smuggler turned knight in the service of King Stannis Baratheon
- Princess Sansa Stark, eldest daughter of Eddard Stark and Catelyn Stark, held captive by the King on the Iron Throne at King's Landing
- Princess Arya Stark, youngest daughter of Eddard Stark and Catelyn Stark, missing and presumed dead
- Prince Bran Stark, second son of Eddard Stark and Catelyn Stark and heir to Winterfell and the Kingdom in the North
- Jon Snow, bastard son of Eddard Stark and a man of the Night's Watch
- Theon Greyjoy, heir to the Seastone Chair and former ward of Lord Eddard Stark
- Queen Daenerys Targaryen, Stormborn, of the Targaryen Dynasty

Translations

- Bulgarian: *"Сблъсък на Крале"*
- Chinese: 重庆出版社(2006): "列王的纷争".
- Croatian: *"Sraz kraljeva"*
- Czech: *Střet králů*
- Dutch: Luitingh-Sijthoff (1999): *"De strijd der koningen"*
- Estonian: Two volumes (Hardcover: Varrak (2008,2009): *"Kuningate heitlus"*
- Finnish: *"Kuninkaiden koitos"*
- French: Three volumes (Hardcover: Pygmalion (2000); paperback: J'ai Lu (2002)): *"La bataille des rois"*, *"L'ombre maléfique"*, *"L'invincible forteresse"*
- German: Single volume, Fantasy Productions (2004): *"Königsfehde"*. Two volumes, Blanvalet (2000): *"Der Thron der Sieben Königreiche"*, *"Die Saat des goldenen Löwen"*.
- Greek: Two volumes, Anubis (2005): *"Σύγκρουση Βασιλέων"*
- Hebrew: עימות המלכים (Two volumes)
- Hungarian: Single volume, Alexandra: *"Királyok csatája"*
- Italian: Two volumes, Mondadori (2002): *"Il regno dei lupi"*, *"La regina dei draghi"*; as a single volume titled "Lo scontro dei re" in the collection Urania Fantasy - Le grandi saghe (July 2008)

- Japanese: 王狼たちの□旗 (The Wolf-King Clan's Battle) Hayakawa Publishing Corporation (2004) Hardcover, 2 volumes; (2007) softcover, 5 volumes.
- Korean: 왕들의 전쟁
- Polish: *"Starcie królów"*
- Portuguese: Two volumes: Saída de Emergência (2008): *"A Fúria dos Reis"*, *"O Despertar da Magia"*
- Romanian: Two volumes: *"Încleştarea Regilor"*
- Russian: Single volume, AST (2004, 2005, 2006): *"Битва королей"*. Two volumes, AST (2000): *"Битва королей. Книга 1"*, *"Битва королей. Книга 2"*.
- Serbian: *"Sudar kraljeva"*
- Slovene: *"Spopad kraljev"* (2008)
- Spanish: Gigamesh (2003): *"Choque de reyes"*
- Swedish: *"Sagan om Eld och Is: Kungarnas Krig"*

Awards and nominations

- Locus Award – Best Novel (Fantasy) (Won) – (1999)
- Nebula Award – Best Novel (Nominated) – (1999)
- Ignotus Award – Best Novel (Foreign) (Won) – (2004)

External links

- A Wiki Of Ice And Fire [2] Wiki dedicated to A Song of Ice and Fire
- *A Clash of Kings* [3] at the Internet Book List
- A Clash of Kings [4] at Worlds Without End

A Storm of Swords

A Storm of Swords	
US Hardcover Edition	
Author	George R. R. Martin
Cover artist	Steve Youll
Country	United States
Language	English
Series	A Song of Ice and Fire
Genre(s)	Fantasy
Publisher	Bantam Spectra (US) & Voyager Books (UK)
Publication date	August 2000 (UK) & November 2000 (US)
Media type	Print (Hardback & Paperback)
Pages	973 (US Hardback), 976 (UK Hardback), 1216 (US Paperback)
ISBN	ISBN 0-553-10663-5 (US Hardback), ISBN 0-00-224586-8 (UK Hardback), ISBN 0-553-57342-X (US Paperback)
OCLC Number	44676135 [1]
Dewey Decimal	813/.54 21
LC Classification	PS3563.A7239 S7 2000
Preceded by	*A Clash of Kings*
Followed by	*A Feast for Crows*

A Storm of Swords is the third of seven planned novels in ***A Song of Ice and Fire***, an epic fantasy series by American author George R. R. Martin. It was first published on 8 August 2000 in the United Kingdom, with a United States edition following in November 2000. Its publication was preceded by a novella called *Path of the Dragon*, which collects some of the Daenerys Targaryen chapters from the novel into a single book.

To date, *A Storm of Swords* is the longest novel in the series. It was so long that in the UK its paperback edition was split in half, Part 1 being published as *Steel and Snow* in June 2001 (with the one-volume cover) and Part 2 as *Blood and Gold* in August 2001 (with a specially-commissioned new cover). In France, the decision was made to cut the novel into four separate editions.

A Storm of Swords won the 2001 Locus Award, the 2002 Geffen Award for Best Novel and was nominated for the 2001 Nebula Award for Best Novel. Significantly, it was the first novel in the series to be nominated for the Hugo Award, one of the two most prestigious awards in science fiction and fantasy publishing, although it lost to J. K. Rowling's novel *Harry Potter and the Goblet of Fire*.

Meisha Merlin, who had previously issued limited, illustrated editions of both *A Game of Thrones* and *A Clash of Kings*, were planning to release a similar version for *A Storm of Swords* in two volumes. However, lengthy delays on the release of *A Clash of Kings* caused Meisha Merlin to lose the printing rights for the book, which were picked up by Subterranean Press instead. This edition, fully illustrated by Charles Vess, was released in the summer of 2006.

A Storm of Swords is also the name of the second expansion to the board game *A Game of Thrones*, released in July 2006.

Plot introduction

The series is set in a fictitious world reminiscent of Medieval Europe, primarily on a continent called Westeros. In this world the seasons can last for many years, sometimes decades.

Plot summary

A Storm of Swords picks up the story slightly before the end of its predecessor, *A Clash of Kings*. The Seven Kingdoms are still in the grip of the War of the Five Kings, with Robb Stark, Balon Greyjoy, Joffrey Baratheon, Stannis Baratheon and Renly Baratheon fighting to secure their crowns. Stannis Baratheon's attempt to take King's Landing has been defeated by the new alliance between House Lannister (backing Joffrey) and House Tyrell. House Martell has also pledged its support to the Lannisters though the forces of Dorne have yet to take the field. Meanwhile, a large host of wildlings is marching on the Wall under Mance Rayder, with only the tiny force of the Night's Watch in its path; and in the distant east, Daenerys Targaryen is on her way back to Pentos in the hope of raising forces to retake the Iron Throne.

The novel begins in the final months of 299 After the Landing and carries on into the year 300 AL.

Note the UK edition of Storm of Swords was split into two books, and the French edition in four. The plot summary below contains information on the original US edition.

In the Seven Kingdoms

The North / The Riverlands

At Riverrun Catelyn Stark strikes a deal with the captive Jaime Lannister: his freedom in return for that of Catelyn's daughters. Jaime agrees, and is sent south, escorted by Brienne of Tarth. Edmure Tully, determined to prove his loyalty to his liege Robb Stark following his failures in the previous novel, reneges on Catelyn's bargain and sends men to hunt Jaime and Brienne.

Jaime spends most of his time insulting Brienne, despite her great size and strength with a sword. They are forced to abandon the river and take to the countryside, but are waylaid by mercenaries from the eastern continent known as The Brave Companions (now in the service of Roose Bolton, having swapped sides from the Lannisters) and taken to Harrenhal, which is now under their command. The leader of the Companions, Vargo Hoat, known for his sadism and cruelty, chops off Jaime's sword hand. But upon being presented to Roose Bolton, Hoat finds his current lord unimpressed by his behavior and Roose sends Jaime back to King's Landing with compliments to Lord Tywin. This strikes all members of the party as an odd thing to do. Brienne, seen as having little leverage as a hostage, is unfortunately left to Hoat's mercies. After Jaime is released, he has a change of heart and comes back to rescue her, helping save her from a bear pit. Roose sees no alternative but to let them both go, and as Jaime leaves, he tells Bolton to "Send Robb Stark my regards."

Robb's army returns to Riverrun in triumph, having smashed several of Lannister forces in the Westerlands. However, Robb is furious with his uncle Edmure: Robb's plan was for Tywin to come west and into a trap Robb was preparing, but Edmure's over-zealous defense of Riverrun spoiled the surprise. Catelyn is shocked when Robb reveals that he has married Jeyne Westerling of the Crag, violating his oath of betrothal to a daughter of House Frey and thus risking losing their support, as their cooperation was contingent upon the promised marriage. This is further aggravated by the fact that the garrison Robb had left behind in the Twins (Frey castle) to ensure their loyalty was withdrawn by Edmure to fight in the Riverlands. Robb claims he had no choice: Jeyne 'comforted' him after he learned of the burning of Winterfell and the deaths of Bran and Rickon. The King in the North is in dire straits: his forces are dwindling due to the imminent loss of the Freys as well as the Karstarks, whose lord Rickard murders two Lannister POWs and is executed as a traitor. Moreover, in a botched attack on Duskendale ordered by Roose Bolton; the force of foot, led by Robett Glover, is caught between Lord Randyll Tarly and Ser Gregor Clegane, leading to the slaughter of a third of Robb's strength. He cannot retreat for more men, as the Greyjoys now hold his home territory. Nevertheless, Robb has a new plan to outflank and take Moat Cailin (via the marshlands surrounding it) from the Greyjoys and allow them to return to the North. Unfortunately, the Riverlords will have to fight on for themselves. Catelyn agrees to this plan, but it hinges on winning the support of the Freys once more, which they are now unlikely to give. Robb is angry that Catelyn let Jaime go, but cunningly uses her guilt at this in order to get her to approve of his marriage to Jeyne Westerling. Not long after this, Lord Hoster Tully finally dies and Edmure becomes Lord of Riverrun.

Arya Stark and her friends encounter a group of men known as the Brotherhood Without Banners, led by Lord Beric Dondarrion and the red priest Thoros of Myr. Beric's group was originally sent out by Lord Eddard to put down the Lannister raids, but have evolved into a Robin Hood-esque organization, defending the smallfolk of the war-torn Riverlands. The group encounters Sandor Clegane, Joffrey's former bodyguard who fled the Battle of the Blackwater, and offer him trial by battle, which he wins (by dealing Lord Beric a killing stroke) and is set free. To Arya's amazement, Thoros is able to resurrect Beric using what he calls a gift from R'hllor. Arya eventually tires of following the Brotherhood and tries to break free, but is captured by a lurking Sandor Clegane instead. Clegane decides to take her back to her family in exchange for some kind of service, and they head north.

Robb Stark's host, now reinforced by Lord Roose Bolton's army from Harrenhal, reaches The Twins, where Robb parleys with Lord Walder Frey. Frey agrees to forgive Robb on the condition that Lord Edmure Tully weds one of Frey's daughters in Robb's place. Edmure's new bride, Roslin, turns out to be an attractive and gentle woman, which surprises Catelyn: the "late Lord Frey" is known for his tetchiness, and could easily have forced Edmure to marry a lackwit or an ugly girl instead. Robb and Catelyn are wary at first, but relax once they are offered food and drink by the Freys which by tradition means they must now be treated and protected as guests. The wedding celebration is held and a great party takes place afterwards, though the food and musicians are described as being terrible. This is forced into perspective when Frey's musicians begin playing "*The Rains of Castamere*", a song celebrating Tywin Lannister's eradication of an unfaithful vassal, produce crossbows and fire into the Stark supporters. The Boltons and Freys, armed and armored, cut down many of the Stark bannermen present, killing Dacey Mormont and Smalljon Umber among them. Catelyn takes one of Walder Frey's grandsons, the halfwit Aegon, hostage with a knife, and threatens to kill him should Robb be harmed, but a man wearing the colours of House Bolton cuts down Robb down anyway, saying "Jaime Lannister sends his regards." Catelyn kills her hostage, but in turn is restrained and her throat cut. In mockery of the Tully burial rites, she is dumped into the river and Robb has his head chopped off and the head of his direwolf, Grey Wind, sewn into its place (as foretold by a vision Daenerys had in the house of the Undying). Many of the northern lords are either killed or taken prisoner, but there are two missing: Robb had sent Lady Maege Mormont and Lord Galbart Glover to win the allegiance of Lord Howland Reed of Greywater Watch for their planned attack on Moat Cailin since only the crannogmen know how to navigate through the swamp.

Arya and Sandor arrive in the outskirts of the castle as the "Red Wedding" is taking place. Soon realizing something is dreadfully wrong, Arya attempts to enter the castle and rescue her mother, Sandor knocks her unconscious with an axe and takes her downriver. Arya then has a dream in which she is actually her long-missing direwolf, Nymeria, who now leads a huge pack of wolves in the Riverlands. In the dream, Nymeria finds the corpse of a woman floating in the Green Fork south of the Twins and pulls it ashore, only to flee as a group of men approach. After this, Arya gives up on her mother, tells The Hound that, in her dream, Catelyn was dead. This is not the first time Arya has had this dream though the other instances were less important.

Arya and Sandor run afoul of some of his brother Gregor Clegane's men in an inn, the Tickler and Polliver along with a squire. There is a fight and the freeriders (two of whom are on Arya's list of people she has vowed to see dead) are killed, but Sandor is wounded. His wound soon becomes infected and Arya refuses to give him the gift of mercy and leaves him dying under a tree and goes to the nearby port town of Saltpans, on the Trident. She finds a ship from the Free City of Braavos there, but they refuse to take her north. She pulls out the coin Jaqen H'ghar gave her and the ship crew suddenly become more cooperative. They won't take her north, but agree to take her back to Braavos with them.

The South / King's Landing

Davos Seaworth is washed ashore on a rocky island in the Narrow Sea, having been nearly killed in the epic Battle of the Blackwater. He is found by bannermen loyal to his Lord Stannis and taken back to Dragonstone. Along the way Davos comes to blame the red priestess Melisandre for Stannis' defeat and resolves to murder her. Upon his arrival he is immediately locked up for treason: Melisandre saw his intent in her flames. Melisandre talks to Davos and claims that Stannis was defeated because she herself was not at the battle (at his bannermen's request), and asks for Davos simply to be true to his king. She also tells him that there are not seven gods but two: R'hllor, Lord of Light and Fire, and his enemy, the Great Other, Lord of Darkness and Cold, whose war has raged since the dawn of time. Stannis releases Davos and asks him to serve as his Hand. Davos agrees and begins to learn to read and write to better fulfill his office.

King's Landing is rejoicing for their deliverance from the threat of Stannis Baratheon and the Tyrells are welcomed as liberators. King Joffrey agrees to set aside his betrothal to Sansa Stark, daughter of a House attainted of treason, and promises to marry Lady Margaery Tyrell instead. Sansa's freedom is short-lived, however, as she is soon compelled to marry Tyrion Lannister. Tyrion was badly injured in the battle, losing his nose and suffering other wounds to his face, but he treats Sansa gently and refuses to consummate the marriage against her will, despite his father's insistence. Tyrion himself is unimpressed with the turn of events, particularly as his father has taken up his role as Hand, reducing Tyrion to an advisory role, although he is later made master of coin to replace Petyr "Littlefinger" Baelish (who has been named Lord of Harrenhal for his role in securing the Lannister-Tyrell alliance). Balon Greyjoy, styling himself King of the Iron Islands and the North, sends an offer of an alliance to Tywin, but Tywin spurns it, as he has another plan that does not involve selling off half the realm. He also comments that he should not pay for what the Greyjoys are already doing for free, that is fighting the Starks.

On Dragonstone, Davos meets Edric Storm, one of King Robert's many bastards whom Stannis is keeping safe from the Lannisters. Davos is horrified to learn that Melisandre wants to sacrifice Edric and his royal blood to her fires to awaken the 'stone dragons,' which she thinks are the great statues that guard the castle. Stannis rejects this decision and instead gives some of his blood to the fires instead, naming the names of three men that he wants dead: Balon Greyjoy, Joffrey Baratheon and Robb Stark. (Chronologically, this happens shortly before the Red Wedding.)

Littlefinger, fresh from his diplomatic victory in gaining the alliance of the Tyrells and the now the titular Lord of Harrenhal, departs King's Landing for the Eyrie with a new scheme: to woo Lady Lysa

Arryn into marriage and support of King Joffrey. Tyrion is suspicious of Littlefinger's growing power but is no longer in a position to stop him.

Word reaches King's Landing of the death of King Robb Stark at the Red Wedding, closely followed by news that King Balon Greyjoy has died as well, swept over a bridge in Pyke by a strong wave. Joffrey is exultant, particularly keen on the gory detail that Robb's direwolf's head was sewn on his body, and Catelyn's body was hurled naked into the Green Fork. Margaery and Joffrey's wedding is held, but Joffrey spends more time tormenting his uncle Tyrion than paying attention to his wife. As he it is relentlessly verbally tormenting Tyrion, Joffrey suddenly starts choking and dies in a fit on the floor. Tyrion suspects poison and inspects Joffrey's goblet before realizing he could be blamed for the crime. He throws the goblet away, but is seen by several witnesses. His sister Cersei has him arrested and put on trial. Sansa Stark is smuggled out of the castle by Ser Dontos, whom she still believes will put her on a ship home. Instead, she discovers that he has sold her to Littlefinger, who plans to take her to the Eyrie with him. Littlefinger also admits to being the mastermind behind Joffrey's death.

Davos Seaworth is learning to read and write. One of the letters he receives is from the Night's Watch, who sent missives to all the kings begging for aid against Mance Rayder and the wights. The success of Melisandre's spell has convinced Stannis to sacrifice Edric Storm to the flames to wake the dragons, but Davos smuggles Edric to safety. Stannis prepares to execute Davos for treason, but as a last wish of sorts Davos is allowed to read the letter that lately arrived from the Wall.

Jaime Lannister and Brienne of Tarth reach King's Landing to find the situation volatile. Joffrey's brother Tommen has inherited the throne but is not yet crowned, Tyrion is on trial, and the Tyrell bannermen blame Brienne for King Renly's death, particularly Renly's brother-in-law Ser Loras Tyrell. She is thrown in a dungeon. Jaime takes up the rank of Lord Commander of the Kingsguard and finds that his journey and the loss of his hand has made him more willing to fulfil his duties. He refuses his father's offer to remove him from his lifetime service to the Kingsguard and again make him heir to Casterly Rock. He also refuses to believe Cersei's claims that Tyrion killed Joffrey. He rejects her advances, deciding to remain true to his vows.

Tyrion is seemingly doomed, as his sister Cersei, convinced of his guilt, has recruited many to give evidence against him, including Varys (master of whisperers, equivalent of the head of intelligence) and Shae (Tyrion's whore). Lord Oberyn Martell of Dorne, who is in the city representing his brother Prince Doran, harbors a desire for vengeance against Gregor Clegane, who it is believed raped his sister Elia (the late wife of Prince Rhaegar Targaryen) and viciously killed her and her children during the Sack of King's Landing. However, Tyrion is approached by Lord Oberyn Martell, who offers to fight for him in a trial of combat against Cersei's champion, who they both know will be Ser Gregor Clegane, "the Mountain that Rides". The battle is fought and surprisingly, Oberyn apparently emerges victorious after knocking the giant Gregor down with a poisoned spear. Unfortunately, he spends too much time gloating and Gregor kills him. Tyrion is condemned to death, but is later helped to escape from his dungeon by his brother Jaime and Varys. On his way out of the castle, Jaime in a bout of guilt, reveals that Tyrion's first wife, whom he loved dearly, had not been a prostitute hired unbeknownst to Tyrion to service him, as their father had told him, but had actually been a crofter's daughter as she appeared. Tyrion sees this as unforgivable betrayal from both his father and his brother; he swears vengeance against both, and carries out the former by stopping at his father's chamber and shooting him with a crossbow. Since his father has taken Shae as a lover, he kills her too, strangling her with the chain of the king's Hand.

Jaime frees Brienne from imprisonment after persuading Loras to reconsider, giving her the sword Lord Tywin had reforged out of Eddard Stark's Valyrian steel blade (after being maimed by Vargo Hoat, Jaime is much less of a swordsman so he believes the blade is wasted on him). He tells her to fulfil the oath she gave to Lady Catelyn, to find Arya and Sansa and return them home. He also tells her that the real reason he betrayed his oath and murdered King Aerys many years back was because Aerys had hidden wildfire barrels all over King's Landing and planned to destroy the city during the Sack. He carried out his most infamous act to save the innocent, not that anyone would believe him. Brienne departs on her quest.

At the Eyrie, Sansa lives in fear of her increasingly psychotic aunt, who eventually goes mad and tries to kill her after she sees Littlefinger kiss her (for which she blames Sansa, not being able to see Littlefinger as culpable). Littlefinger intervenes to save Sansa, and then after deftly mollifying Lysa, he unceremoniously pushes her out of the 'moon door' of the Eyrie to her death hundreds of feet below and blames Lysa's minstrel for the crime. However, before her death, Sansa hears Lysa reveal that Littlefinger told her to poison Jon Arryn and blame the Lannisters in a letter sent to her sister Catelyn many months before.

In the epilogue, Merrett Frey goes to a parley with a group from the Brotherhood Without Banners, who have taken one of his brothers "Petyr Pimple" captive and are demanding a ransom. During the parley the Brothers reveal that they have executed the other Frey he came to free. They point out to the panicking Merrett that he was at the Red Wedding and helped in the murder of the guests. He demands that they prove it by providing a witness. In response a battered figure appears and points at him. Merrett Frey is hanged next to the corpses of his family, whilst the broken and mute form of Catelyn Stark watches, and hates.

On the Wall

The bulk of the strength of the Night's Watch sits on the Fist of the First Men, awaiting word from Qhorin Halfhand and Jon Snow. Suddenly three blasts are sounded on a watchman's horn, which means something not heard in nearly eight thousand years: Others. The Watch comes under attack by wights and the fabled ice demons of ancient history, but manages to withdraw in something approaching good order. Samwell Tarly kills one of the Others with a strange blade Jon Snow fashioned for him from obsidian, or "dragonglass," he found near the Fist. The Watch regroups at Craster's Keep, but some of the less respectable members of the Watch mutiny and kill Lord Commander Jeor Mormont. Sam escapes in the chaos with the help of one of Craster's daughter-wives, Gilly, and they make their way south towards the Wall. They meet and are helped by a strange figure riding an elk, who Sam calls 'Coldhands'.

Jon Snow is taken to Mance Rayder and is able to convince him that he has truly turned his cloak. He learns that the fabled Others have returned and are driving the wildlings south towards the Wall. Mance has been seeking the legendary Horn of Winter which will shatter the Wall when sounded, but has been unable to find it. Jon is unsure of this story. Eventually, Jon is sent south on a mission to scale the Wall, circle around, and attack Castle Black from the south to allow the wildlings through the gates. Jon instead flees from the wildlings and reaches Castle Black to warn them of the threat. He learns that Bowen Marsh has taken most of the remaining garrison with him as he attempts to repel wildling attacks all along the Wall (that are really feints). With many of the other Watch members dead or missing, Jon is forced to command a skeleton defense along with villagers fleeing from Mole Town against the wildlings, but nevertheless successfully repels them for the time being. Among the dead is the wilding Ygritte, who had been Jon's lover for a time, despite his oath of celibacy.

Bran Stark and Jojen and Meera Reed, fleeing the ruins of Winterfell, are guided north by Bran's strange dreams of a three-eyed crow. They reach the Wall at the abandoned castle of the Nightfort, but cannot pass it. Miraculously the gate opens and they meet Samwell Tarly and Gilly. Sam guides them to Coldhands, who will take them north, whilst Sam returns to Castle Black, agreeing to keep the truth of their survival a secret.

The wildling army, over forty thousand strong, reaches Castle Black and assaults the Wall at that location. Jon leads a tenacious defence which sees hundreds of wildlings killed, but it seems that the Watch must be overrun. Things get worse when Janos Slynt, the former commander of King's Landing's City Watch who was exiled by a suspicious Tyrion Lannister, arrives. As one of the betrayers of Eddard Stark, Slynt takes an instant dislike to Jon Snow and accuses him of being a traitor. He has Jon sent out to parley with Mance Rayder. Jon expects to be killed, but Rayder is more understanding of his betrayal. Jon is shocked to learn that Rayder found the Horn of Winter, but would rather climb the Wall with it than melt it: with the Wall gone, what will stop the Others? Suddenly horns are heard in the east and a great strength of cavalry from seemingly out of nowhere attacks the wildling army, plunging it into chaos and putting it to rout. To Jon's disbelief, the surviving army of King Stannis Baratheon has arrived. Rayder is captured and imprisoned. Stannis reveals that he received word of the Wall's dire straits (the letter Ser Davos Seaworth read) and that Melisandre believes the wildling invasion to be the forerunner of the return of The Other, the sworn foe of the red god R'hllor. Stannis resolves to forge a new kingdom out of the shattered, leaderless North, and as part of this plan offers to make Jon Snow rightful heir to the North, removing his bastardy and anointing him the Lord of Winterfell. Jon is torn over this offer, which would grant him what has always been his deepest desire - to be a Stark. In place, he would have to cast out the old gods he has worshiped all his life. However, his internal debate is rendered moot when he is unexpectedly chosen by the Night's Watch as its new

Lord Commander, through the clever machinations of Samwell Tarly, who along with many comrades was very worried about what would happen to the Watch if the increasingly popular Slynt were to be chosen.

In the East

Returning to Pentos by sea, Daenerys Targaryen learns from Ser Jorah Mormont that large slave armies that could be used in her quest to retake her family's throne in Westeros can be bought in the cities of Slaver's Bay in the region of Ghis: Meereen, Astapor and Yunkai. To Arstan Whitebeard's disgust—slavery has been illegal in the Seven Kingdoms for millennia—Daenerys agrees to give up one of her beloved infant dragons to entice the Slavers to sell her the entire host of the Unsullied, the feared warrior-eunuchs of Astapor. After the command is given to the slaves declaring Daenerys their new master, the very dragon that was to be given to the Slavers burns them alive, and Daenerys' small host and the newly acquired Unsullied, sack the city. Daenerys has all the slaves of Astapor set free. She leads a strong force north to Yunkai which forces the lords of the city to release their slaves into Daenerys' service. However, the lords of Meereen choose to antagonise Daenerys by killing 163 (by her count) of their child slaves and leaving one corpse staked at every mile along the road to the city while using the scorched earth technique to deny her resources. Daenerys besieges the city to no avail.

Daenerys discovers two traitors in her camp: Ser Jorah Mormont and Arstan Whitebeard. However, the nature of their treachery is very different. Mormont was selling information about her to Robert Baratheon up until they reached Qarth. Arstan Whitebeard is actually an alias of Ser Barristan Selmy, former Lord Commander of the Kingsguard. Barristan wanted to right the decades past wrong of accepting Robert as his king by finding the true Targaryen heir to Westeros, but wanted to make sure the taint of madness had not affected her as it had her father and siblings. Daenerys offers both men the chance to make amends: by sneaking into Meereen through its sewers and opening the gates. In the meantime, she uses her three ships as battering rams to distract the defenders while Barristan and Jorah free the slaves in the fighting pits, setting off an uprising in which Meereen soon falls. She forgives Barristan Selmy and makes him Lord Commander of her Queensguard. However, she finds she still cannot trust Mormont and has him banished from her presence. Learning that Astapor has fallen under the control of a brutal dictator who moved to fill the power vacuum she left behind, Daenerys decides she cannot allow that to happen to Meereen and resolves to stay, and rule, and learn to be the queen that Westeros needs her to be.

Characters

The tale is told through the eyes of 10 main characters, a one-off prologue POV and a one-off epilogue POV character (the only time this has been done in the series so far):

- Prologue: Chett, a brother and hound-keeper of the Night's Watch.
- Ser Jaime Lannister, eldest son of Tywin Lannister, brother of Tyrion Lannister, held captive by the King in the North at Riverrun
- Jon Snow, bastard son of Eddard Stark. A sworn brother of the Night's Watch
- Lady Catelyn Stark, of House Tully, widow of Lord Eddard Stark
- Tyrion Lannister, youngest son of Tywin Lannister, a dwarf, brother of Ser Jaime Lannister
- Princess Sansa Stark, eldest daughter of Eddard Stark and Catelyn Stark, held captive by the King on the Iron Throne at King's Landing
- Princess Arya Stark, youngest daughter of Eddard and Catelyn Stark, missing and presumed dead
- Prince Bran Stark, son of Eddard and Catelyn Stark, Prince of Winterfell, heir to the North, believed dead
- Samwell Tarly, fat and cowardly son of Lord Tarly and a sworn brother of the Night's Watch; also the former heir to Horn Hill
- Ser Davos Seaworth, a smuggler turned knight in the service of King Stannis Baratheon
- Queen Daenerys Targaryen, Stormborn, of the Targaryen Dynasty
- Epilogue: Merrett Frey, a member of the numerous Frey family.

Notes

George R. R. Martin did not write the Red Wedding chapters until he had completed every other chapter of the book, as he felt it was a painful experience to write.

George R. R. Martin lost the 2001 Hugo Award for Best Novel to J. K. Rowling.[*citation needed*] Afterwards he made this comment about his fans: "Eat your heart out, Rowling. Maybe you have billions of dollars and my Hugo, but you don't have readers like these."

The Brotherhood Without Banners, introduced in *A Storm of Swords* but referenced in earlier novels, also became the name of the official George R. R. Martin fan group. The name was adopted in the first half of 2001, and the group held its first major gathering at the 2001 World Science Fiction Convention in Philadelphia.[*citation needed*]

On October 6, 2009, Martin noted on his blog that his manuscript for *A Storm of Swords* had been 1521 pages in length; the initial printed hardcover came in at 992 pages.

Allusions and references to other works

A character named Trebor Jordayne of the Tor is mentioned in *A Storm of Swords*; Tor Books is the best-known publisher of fantasy author Robert Jordan, and "Trebor" is "Robert" backwards. A ship named the *Cobblecat* is noted as the vessel Davos Seaworth had been sailing on when he first saw the Wall; Martin's short story "A Beast For Norn" features a cobalt panther, called a "cobalcat."

Translations

- Bulgarian: Bard (2001): *"Вихър от Мечове"*.
- Chinese: 重庆出版社(2007): *"冰雨的风暴"*.
- Croatian: *"Oluja mačeva"*
- Czech: *Bouře mečů*
- Dutch: Two volumes, Luitingh-Sijthoff (2001, 2002): *"Een storm van zwaarden 3A"*, *"Een storm van zwaarden 3B"*
- Finnish: Two volumes, Kirjava (2005, 2006): *"Miekkamyrsky 1"*, *"Miekkamyrsky 2"*
- French: Four volumes (Hardcover: Pygmalion (2001, 2002, 2003); paperback: J'ai Lu (2003, 2004)): *"Les brigands"* (hardcover) / *"Intrigues à Port-Réal"* (paperback), *"L'épée de feu"*, *"Les noces pourpres"*, *"La loi du régicide"*
- German: Single volume, Fantasy Productions (2005): *"Schwertgewitter"*. Two volumes, Blanvalet (2001, 2002): *"Sturm der Schwerter"*, *"Die Königin der Drachen"*.
- Greek: Two volumes, Anubis (2006, 2007): *"Θύελλα απο Ατσάλι"*.
- Hebrew: סופת החרבות (Two volumes)
- Hungarian: Single volume, Alexandra: *"Kardok vihara"*
- Italian: Three volumes, Mondadori (2002, 2003): *"Tempesta di spade"*, *"I fiumi della guerra"*, *"Il portale delle tenebre"*.
- Japanese "剣嵐の大地" (The Vast Land of the Sword-Storm) HC 2006-2007, three volumes. Hayakawa Publishing Corporation
- Korean: "검의 폭풍"
- Polish: Two volumes, Zysk i Ska (both 2002): *"Nawałnica mieczy: Stal i śnieg"*, *"Nawałnica mieczy: Krew i złoto"*
- Portuguese: Two volumes: Saída de Emergência (2008): *"A Tormenta de Espadas"*, *"A Glória dos Traidores"*
- Russian: *"Буря мечей"*
- Serbian: *"Oluja mačeva"*
- Slovene: *"Vihra mečev"* (2010)
- Spanish: Two volumes, Gilgamesh (2005): *"Tormenta de espadas I"*, *"Tormenta de espadas II"*.
- Swedish: Three volumes,*"Kampen om Järntronen"* (1997, 2005), *"Kungarnas Krig"* (2006), *"Svärdets makt"* (2007)

Awards and nominations

- Hugo Award – Best Novel (Nominated) – (2001)
- Locus Award – Best Novel (Fantasy) (Won) – (2001)
- Nebula Award – Best Novel (Nominated) – (2001)
- Geffen Award – Best Fantasy Book (Won) – (2002)
- Ignotus Award – Best Novel (Foreign) (Won) – (2006)

External links

- A Wiki Of Ice And Fire [2] Wiki dedicated to A Song of Ice and Fire
- *A Storm of Swords* [2] at the Internet Book List
- A Storm of Swords [3] at Worlds Without End

A Feast for Crows

A Feast for Crows	
US hardcover edition	
Author	George R. R. Martin
Country	United States
Language	English
Series	*A Song of Ice and Fire*
Genre(s)	Fantasy
Publisher	Voyager Books (UK) Bantam Spectra (US)
Publication date	17 October 2005 (UK) 8 November 2005 (US)
Media type	Print (Hardback & Paperback)
Pages	704 (UK hardback), 753 (US hardback), 1104 (US paperback)
ISBN	ISBN 0-00-224743-7 (UK hardback), ISBN 0-553-80150-3 (US hardback), ISBN 0-553-58202-X (US paperback)
OCLC Number	61261403 [1]
Dewey Decimal	813/.54 22
LC Classification	PS3563.A7239 F39 2005
Preceded by	*A Storm of Swords*
Followed by	*A Dance with Dragons (forthcoming)*

A Feast for Crows is the fourth of seven planned novels in the epic fantasy series *A Song of Ice and Fire* by American author George R. R. Martin. The novel was first published on 17 October 2005 in the United Kingdom, with a United States edition following on 8 November 2005.

In May 2005 Martin announced that the "sheer size" of his still-unfinished manuscript for *A Feast for Crows* had led him and his publishers to split the narrative into two books. Rather than divide the text in half chronologically, Martin opted to instead split the material by character and location, resulting in "two novels taking place simultaneously" with different casts of characters. *A Feast for Crows* was published months later, and the concurrent novel *A Dance with Dragons* is still unreleased as of 2010. Martin also noted that the *A Song of Ice and Fire* series would now likely total seven novels.

A Feast for Crows was the first novel in the sequence to debut at number one on *The New York Times* Best Seller list, a feat among fantasy writers only previously achieved by Robert Jordan and Neil Gaiman. In 2006 the novel was nominated for the Hugo Award, the Locus Award, and the British Fantasy Society Award.

Plot introduction

Set in a fictitious world reminiscent of Medieval Europe in which magic exists and the seasons can last for many years, the *Song of Ice and Fire* series follows the violent dynastic struggles of an empire in turmoil. *A Feast of Crows* continues the events of *A Storm of Swords* (2000), the third novel in the series, and its plot runs concurrently with that of the forthcoming novel *A Dance with Dragons*.

Plot summary

The War of the Five Kings is coming to an end. Robb Stark, Joffrey Baratheon, Renly Baratheon, and Balon Greyjoy are all dead, and King Stannis Baratheon has gone to the aid of the Wall, where Jon Snow has become Lord Commander of the Night's Watch. King Tommen Baratheon, Joffrey's eight-year-old brother, now rules in King's Landing under the watchful eye of his mother, the Queen Regent Cersei Lannister. Cersei's father Tywin is dead, murdered by his son Tyrion, who has fled the city. With both men gone, there are no more checks on Cersei, and she stands at the height of power. Meanwhile, Sansa Stark is still in hiding in the Vale, protected by Petyr Baelish, who has secretly murdered his wife Lysa Arryn and named himself Protector of the Vale and guardian of eight-year-old Lord Robert Arryn.

It soon becomes apparent that while Cersei is skilled in the methods of intrigue needed to seize power, she is not very skilled in the actual day-to-day running of the kingdom. Cersei's reign is marked by rampant cronyism as she tries to solidify her rule by staffing her councils with incompetent loyalists. Making matters worse is Cersei's increasing distrust of the Tyrells, particularly her son's new wife Margaery. Increasingly paranoid over a prophecy she believes foretells the deaths of her children and herself by the hands of her missing brother Tyrion, Cersei develops a dependency on alcohol. Her reign runs into problems from massive war debt, compounded by her incompetent administrators inability to resolve the situation, which leads to a banking crisis that nearly cripples the economy of Westeros. To settle the crown's debts to the Faith, she agrees to the restoration of that religion's military order, the Faith Militant. A scheme to have the Faith put Margaery on trial for largely-invented accusations on adultery goes wrong when the newly-powerful religious leadership arrests and imprisons Cersei herself on similar (and accurate) charges.

Cersei's brother and ex-lover Jaime travels the riverlands to re-establish order and royal control in the war-torn region. He has become somewhat estranged from his sister and newly concerned with his own honor, which he believes is tarnished by past misdeeds. After ending the siege of Riverrun, one of the last holdouts against his family's authority, he receives word that Cersei wants him to return and defend her in a trial by battle, but burns and apparently ignores the message.

On the Iron Islands, Euron Greyjoy is chosen king due to his promise that he can summon dragons that will help the islanders conquer all of Westeros. He sends his brother Victarion east to woo Daenerys Targaryen, but a bitter Victarion instead plans to marry her himself. Meanwhile, in Dorne, a bold attempt by Arianne Martell to crown Myrcella Baratheon as queen of Westeros under Dornish law is thwarted by Arianne's father Doran. The attempt has also left Myrcella's face scarred, straining the new allegiance with House Lannister and the Iron Throne, even as a member of the Kingsguard is on his way to Dorne with the head of Gregor Clegane, a knight blamed for the murder of Doran's daughter Elia years before. Though angry with his Arianne, Doran reveals to her that he has long had his own subtler plan for vengeance; her brother Quentyn has gone east to bring back "Fire and blood."

Brienne of Tarth's quest for Sansa leads her all over the riverlands, where she observes the devastation and villainy that the war has wrought among the smallfolk. Eventually captured by the Brotherhood Without Banners, she is sentenced to death by her former ally, now corpse-like Catelyn Stark, who wrongly believes Brienne has betrayed her. Brienne is told she will be allowed to live if she agrees to find and kill Jaime Lannister; refusing, she and some of her companions are hanged, and as the nooses strangle them she screams out one as-yet unrevealed word.

Samwell Tarly is sent to the Citadel in Oldtown for training to become a Maester and to learn what the Maesters know of the Others. Accompanied by Maester Aemon, Dareon (another man of the Night's Watch), and the wildling girl Gilly, Sam travels to Braavos, where Aemon's ill health causes them to miss their boat and Dareon loses interest in their mission. Sam, Aemon, and Gilly eventually resume their voyage to Oldtown, but en route Aemon dies and Sam and Gilly become lovers. Finally, at Oldtown, Sam becomes a novice, and a Maester leaves to try and offer counsel to Daenerys, whom Aemon had believed is the promised savior of mankind.

Arriving in Braavos, Arya Stark finds her way to the House of Black and White, a temple associated with the assassins known as the Faceless Men. As a novice there, Arya attempts to master their belief that Faceless Men have no true identity by posing as a girl named "Cat of the Canals", however, her former identity somewhat asserts itself when she kills Dareon on principle for abandoning the Night's Watch (Which anywhere on Westeros is punishable by death) and also for abandoning his sworn brother Samwell Tarly who Arya had come to have a passing acquaintance with. The morning after her return to the House of Black and White following this murder, she admits that it was "Arya" who committed it, and is therefore given a glass of milk meant for "Arya" as punishment. After drinking, she wakes up blind the following morning.

In the Eyrie, Sansa poses as Petyr's bastard daughter Alayne, befriending young Robert Arryn, managing the household for her "father," and receiving informal training in royal politics from him. During this time, Petyr appears to be carefully manipulating his murdered wife's former bannermen, and his once precarious hold on the Protectorship Vale is beginning to seem less tenuous. He eventually reveals that he has betrothed Sansa to Harrold Hardyng, Robert's heir; when the sickly

Robert dies, Sansa will reveal her true identity, and reclaim her family stronghold of Winterfell.

Characters

The story is narrated from the point of view of 12 characters and, as with previous volumes, a one-off prologue point of view of a relatively minor character.

- Prologue: Pate, a novice of the Maesters in Oldtown
- Cersei Lannister, The Queen Regent
- The Prophet, The Drowned Man: Aeron "Damphair" Greyjoy
- Jaime Lannister, Lord Commander of the Kingsguard
- The Captain of the Guards: Areo Hotah, Captain of Guards to Prince Doran Martell of Dorne
- Arya Stark, later referred to as "Cat of the Canals", beginning her training by the House of Black and White (The Faceless Men)
- Sansa Stark, pretending to be Petyr Baelish's bastard daughter "Alayne Stone" (by which name her later chapters are known)
- Samwell Tarly, a sworn brother of the Night's Watch
- The Kraken's Daughter: Asha Greyjoy, daughter of King Balon of the Iron Islands
- The Iron Captain, The Reaver: Victarion Greyjoy, King Balon's brother
- Brienne of Tarth, an unnaturally huge and muscled young woman searching for Sansa and Arya Stark
- The Soiled Knight: Arys Oakheart of the Kingsguard
- The Queenmaker, The Princess in the Tower: Arianne Martell, daughter of Prince Doran

Publication

Martin released the first four "Iron Islands" chapters of *A Feast for Crows* as a novella called *Arms of the Kraken*, published in the August 2002 edition of *Dragon* magazine. Another chapbook featuring three Daenerys chapters was published for BookExpo 2005, although these chapters were subsequently moved into the forthcoming fifth volume in the series, *A Dance with Dragons*.

Martin originally planned for the fourth book to be called *A Dance with Dragons* with the story picking up five years after the events of *A Storm of Swords* (primarily to advance the ages of the younger characters). However, during the writing process it was discovered that this was leading to an overreliance on flashbacks to fill in the gap. After twelve months or so of working on the book, Martin decided to abandon much of what had previously been written and start again, this time picking up immediately after the end of *A Storm of Swords*. He announced this decision, along with the new title *A Feast for Crows*, at Worldcon in Philadelphia on September 1, 2001. He also announced that *A Dance with Dragons* would now be the fifth book in the sequence.

In May 2005 Martin announced that his manuscript for *A Feast for Crows* had hit 1527 completed pages but still remained unfinished, with "another hundred or so pages of roughs and incomplete chapters, as well as other chapters sketched out but entirely unwritten." As the size of the manuscript for 2000's *A Storm of Swords*, his previous novel, had been a problem for publishers around the world at 1521 pages, Martin and his publishers had decided to split the narrative planned for *A Feast for Crows* into two books. Rather than divide the text in half chronologically, Martin opted to instead split the material by character and location:

> It was my feeling ... that we were better off telling all the story for half the characters, rather than half the story for all the characters. Cutting the novel in half would have produced two half-novels; our approach will produce two novels taking place simultaneously, but set hundreds or even thousands of miles apart, and involving different casts of characters (with some overlap).

Martin noted that *A Feast for Crows* would focus on "Westeros, King's Landing, the riverlands, Dorne, and the Iron Islands," and that the next novel, *A Dance with Dragons*, would cover "events in the east and north." Martin also added that the *A Song of Ice and Fire* series would now likely total seven novels. *A Feast for Crows* was published months later on 17 October 2005, over five years after the previous volume in the series, *A Storm of Swords*. The parallel novel *A Dance with Dragons* is still unreleased as of 2010.

Allusions and references to other works

In *A Feast for Crows*, Martin names the god Bakkalon, the Pale Child, as the deity worshipped mostly by soldiers at the House of Black and White in Braavos; Bakkalon is also a god in Martin's 1975 story "And Seven Times Never Kill Man" and in other stories of the same era. In the chapter titled "The Kraken's Daughter," Rodrik Harlaw mentions an Archmaester named Rigney who believes that history is a wheel. *The Wheel of Time* fantasy series author Robert Jordan's real name is James Rigney.

Release details

- 2005, UK, Voyager ISBN 0-00-224743-7, Pub date 17 October 2005, hardback
- 2005, UK, Voyager ISBN 0-00-722463-X, Pub date ? ? 2005, hardback (presentation edition)
- 2005, US, Spectra Books ISBN 0-553-80150-3, Pub date 8 November 2005, hardback
- 2006, UK, Voyager ISBN 0-00-224742-9, Pub date 25 April 2006, paperback

Translations

- Bulgarian: Bard (2006): *"Пир за Врани"*
- Chinese (Simplified): 重庆出版社(2008): *"群鸦的盛宴"*
- Chinese (Traditional): 高寶國際(2006): *"群鴉盛宴"*
- Croatian: Algoritam (2006): *"Gozba vrana"*
- Dutch: Luitingh (2006): *"Een feestmaal voor kraaien"*
- Finnish: *"Korppien kestit"* (2007)
- French: Hardcover: Pygmalion (2006-...): *"Le chaos"*, *"Les sables de Dorne"*, *"Un Festin pour les Corbeaux"*
- German: Single volume, Fantasy Productions (2006): *"Krähenfest"* (to be released). Two volumes, Blanvalet (2006): *"Zeit der Krähen"*, *"Die dunkle Königin"*
- Greek: Two volumes, Anubis (2007, 2008): *"Βορά Ορνίων"*
- Hungarian: Alexandra (2007): *"Varjak lakomája"*
- Italian: *"Il Dominio della Regina"* (Volume 1, 2006), *"L'ombra della profezia"* (Volume 2, 2007)
- Japanese: 乱鴉の饗宴 (*The War-Crow's Feast*) 2008, Hardcover, 2 volumes, Hayakawa Publishing Corporation
- Polish: *"Uczta dla wron"*
- Portuguese: Two volumes: Saída de Emergência (2009): *"O Festim de Corvos"*, *"O Mar de Ferro"*
- Romanian: *"Festinul Ciorilor"*
- Russian: *"Пир стервятников"*
- Serbian: Laguna (2006): *"Гозба за вране"*
- Spanish: Gigamesh (2007): *"Festín de Cuervos"*
- Hebrew: Opus (2007): *"משתה לעורבים"*

Awards and nominations

- Hugo Award – Best Novel (nominated) – (2006)
- Locus Award for Fantasy – Best Novel (nominated) – (2006)
- British Fantasy Award – Best Novel (nominated) – (2006)
- Quill Award – Best Novel (Science Fiction & Fantasy) (nominated) – (2006)

References

- Zimmerman, W. Frederick (December 15, 2005) (Paperback). *Unauthorized A Feast for Crows Analysis*. Nimble Books. ISBN 0-9765406-1-4.

External links

- Official website [3] of author George R. R. Martin
- *A Song of Ice and Fire* [1] series listing at the Internet Speculative Fiction Database
- "Worlds Without End: *A Feast for Crows*" [2]. WorldsWithoutEnd.com.

A Dance with Dragons

A Dance with Dragons	
Author	George R. R. Martin
Cover artist	Jamie S. Warren Youll
Country	United States
Language	English
Series	*A Song of Ice and Fire*
Genre(s)	Fantasy
Publisher	Voyager Books (UK) & Spectra Books (USA)
Publication date	To be determined
Media type	Print (Hardcover & Paperback)
Pages	To be determined
ISBN	ISBN 0553801473 (978-0553801477)
OCLC Number	191922936 [1]
Preceded by	*A Feast for Crows*
Followed by	*The Winds of Winter (forthcoming)*

A Dance with Dragons is the fifth of seven planned novels in the epic fantasy series *A Song of Ice and Fire* by American author George R. R. Martin. Although some publishers have listed provisional release dates, after several previously announced dates were not achieved, Martin has indicated that no release date will be set until the book is finished.

A Dance with Dragons was originally the title of the second novel in the sequence, when Martin still envisioned the series as a trilogy. Some early US editions of *A Game of Thrones* (1996) list *A Dance of Dragons* as the forthcoming second volume in the series. The 1998 anthology *Legends*, which features the novella *The Hedge Knight* from the same universe, lists *A Dance of Dragons* as the fourth installment of the series.

Plot introduction

Set in a fictitious world reminiscent of Medieval Europe in which magic exists and the seasons can last for many years, the *Song of Ice and Fire* series follows the violent dynastic struggles of an empire in turmoil. *A Dance with Dragons* continues the events of *A Storm of Swords* (2000), the third novel in the series. The first part of the book runs concurrently with that of its predecessor, *A Feast for Crows* (2005), while the second is set afterwards and will give resolution to some of the storylines begun in *A Feast for Crows*.

Plot summary

The War of the Five Kings in Westeros seems to be winding down. In the North, self-declared King Stannis Baratheon has installed himself at the Wall and vowed to win the support of the northmen to continue his struggle to claim the Iron Throne from the supposed children of his dead brother Robert Baratheon, actually offspring of incest between Robert's wife Cersei Lannister and her twin brother, Jaime the Kingslayer; this is complicated by the fact that much of the west coast is under occupation by the Ironborn. On the Wall itself, Eddard Stark's bastard son Jon Snow has been elected the 998th Lord Commander of the Night's Watch, but the young man has enemies both in the Watch and beyond the Wall, where the armies of Mance Rayder are amassing for an assault. Dwarf Tyrion Lannister has been wrongfully condemned to death for the murder of his young nephew, King Joffrey Baratheon, and has fled by ship across the narrow sea to Pentos, but not before murdering his hated father Tywin. In the far east, Daenerys Targaryen — sole heir to the deposed ruling family, the Targaryens — has conquered the city of Meereen, and rules it to hone her skills of leadership before she moves on to take back Westeros. But her presence is now known to many, and from the Iron Islands and Dorne, from Oldtown and the Free Cities, emissaries are on their way to find Daenerys and use her cause for their own ends.

As early as 2006, Martin made sample chapters available on his website. and at Amazon.co.uk.

Characters

The story is narrated from the point of view of at least 11 characters and, as with previous volumes, a one-off prologue point of view of a relatively minor character.

- Varamyr Sixskins (Prologue), a skinchanger and one of the surviving wildlings north of the Wall.
- Jon Snow, the 998th Lord Commander of the Night's Watch and bastard son of Eddard Stark.
- Tyrion Lannister, dwarf and maternal uncle to the King Tommen of Westeros, a fugitive wanted for kinslaying and regicide. Recently fled the Seven Kingdoms and headed towards the Free Cities.
- Daenerys Targaryen, sole heir to the Targaryen dynasty who ruled Westeros for 300 years until their deposition 15 years prior to the first novel. Called "Stormborn," "the Unburnt," "the Breaker of Shackles," "the Mother of Dragons," and self-proclaimed Queen of Westeros, she now rules the city of Meereen.

- Davos Seaworth, former smuggler and King's Hand to Stannis Baratheon.
- Quentyn Martell (The Merchant's Man), eldest son of Prince Doran Martell of Dorne, traveling into the east on a mission for his father.
- Bran Stark, rightful heir to his brother, the late Robb Stark. Seeking an old power beyond the Wall, believed dead by his own family.
- Asha Greyjoy (The Kraken's Daughter, The Wayward Bride), niece of King Euron Greyjoy of the Iron Islands, lately fled from the isles.
- Theon Greyjoy (Reek), presumed-dead son of recently deceased King Balon Greyjoy of the Iron Islands, a captive of Ramsay Bolton and now tortured, starved and barely sane.
- Arya Stark, hiding in the Free City of Braavos, where she is also called "Cat of the Canals" and continues her training as an assassin by the House of Black and White (The Faceless Men). Meanwhile back in Westeros, an impostor Arya has been betrothed to Ramsay Bolton.
- Lady Melisandre, a mysterious shadow-binder from Asshai and a devoted priestess to the red god R'hllor, adviser to Stannis.
- Cersei Lannister, The Queen Regent, currently imprisoned in a tower cell awaiting trial.
- Another, as yet unrevealed point of view. It is possible that this character was Aeron Damphair, as Martin has stated that his one chapter in *A Dance with Dragons* has been moved to *The Winds of Winter*.
- An epilogue character

In a progress update on his website dated January 1, 2008, Martin said he would add "some chapters from the point of view of one of the characters featured in the first lot of *Ice & Fire* miniatures from Dark Sword, a character who has never had a POV in any of the earlier books". The three characters that met these criteria were Melisandre, Sandor Clegane, and Loras Tyrell. Martin later ruled out Sandor, and on October 17, 2009, he confirmed that Melisandre has at least one point of view chapter in the book.

A Dance with Dragons takes place simultaneously alongside the story of A Feast for Crows, the North, the Free Cities and Slaver's Bay will be featured. GRRM has let it be known that more POV characters will perish in the last 3 remaining books, but not necessarily in ADWD.

Split in publication

According to Martin, his manuscript for the fourth novel in the series had become too large to publish in a single volume. Rather than simply split it in half and publish it as essentially "Part 1" and "Part 2," Martin decided to split the book by character and location. Published in 2005, *A Feast for Crows* is narrated primarily by characters in the South of the Seven Kingdoms and in the new locations of the Iron Islands and Dorne. Characters in the North and across the narrow sea will be featured in *A Dance with Dragons*, although Arya Stark and Asha Greyjoy will appear in both volumes.[*citation needed*]

Approximately one-third of the published *A Dance with Dragons* will consist of material that had been written for the pre-split *A Feast for Crows*, although much of this has been rewritten by Martin.

In 2009, Martin confirmed that, contrary to earlier statements, Sansa Stark will not appear in *A Dance with Dragons*; Sansa chapters initially slated for the novel have instead been pushed back to *The Winds of Winter*, which is planned to be the sixth book in the series. In early 2010, Martin noted that his intent for *A Dance with Dragons* was for the first 800 manuscript pages to cover the alternate characters in the same time span as *A Feast for Crows*, and that "Everything that follows is post-*Feast*, so that's where some of the cast from the last book start popping up again." Stating that "I wanted to resolve at least a few of the cliffhangers from *Feast*," Martin also mentioned the possibility that some of his finished chapters might get pushed to the next novel, *The Winds of Winter*, depending on the length of the finished manuscript for *A Dance with Dragons*.

Delays in publication

Despite original predictions of possible completion in late 2006, Martin has not finished the book as of October 2010. Martin's blog has featured sporadic updates on his progress, and in January 2008 he posted an update on his website affirming his vigilant commitment to finishing the book. In early 2008, publisher Spectra Books (a division of Random House) announced that *A Dance with Dragons* would be released on September 30, 2008, but Martin stated this would only be possible if he finished writing by the end of June, before a trip to Spain and Portugal, and he did not meet this goal.

On February 19, 2009, Martin posted on his website, "I am trying to finish the book by June. I think I can do that. If I do, *A Dance with Dragons* will likely be published in September or October." On June 22, 2009, the author expressed "guarded optimism" in respect to his progress on the book, while still not confirming a publication date. When asked in a July 2009 interview with *FREE! Magazine* how the book was going, Martin stated, "It is going pretty well, actually. I am hoping to finish it by September or October; that is my goal." On October 6, 2009, Martin said that his working manuscript for *A Dance With Dragons* had just exceeded 1,100 pages of completed chapters, plus "considerably more in partials, fragments, and roughs." He noted that this made the upcoming novel longer than his earlier books *A Game of Thrones* and *A Feast for Crows*, and nearly as long as *A Clash of Kings*.

On March 2, 2010, Martin remarked that he had reached 1,311 manuscript pages, making *Dance* the second longest book in the series at that point, behind only the 1,521-page manuscript of *A Storm of Swords*.

On July 8, 2010, Martin spoke at a conference and confirmed the current length of the book to be 1,400 manuscript pages. He expressed his disappointment that he was unable to completely finish the book by the conference, although he would not speculate how soon the book would be completed after his return home on July 11. At the same conference, Martin also confirmed that he has written one Sansa, one Arya, and two Arianne chapters for the planned sixth novel, *Winds of Winter*, and has transferred two Cersei chapters from that book into *A Dance with Dragons*.

On August 7, 2010, Martin confirmed that he has completed 8 POV's, excluding prologue and epilogue.

On October 10, 2010, at the New York Comic Con, Spectra senior editor Anne Groell states that Martin has announced he has five chapters remaining, with sections of the chapters already completed. She also wants to get the manuscript completed by December.

The delays surrounding *A Dance with Dragons* have polarized some of Martin's fan base, questioning his commitment to finishing the series.

External links

- The latest info [2] regarding the completion of *A Dance with Dragons*
- Official website [3] of author George R. R. Martin
- *A Song of Ice and Fire* [1] series listing at the Internet Speculative Fiction Database

The Novellas

Tales of Dunk and Egg

The **Tales of Dunk and Egg** is a series of novellas written by George R. R. Martin, set in the world of his Song of Ice and Fire cycle. Three novellas have appeared so far: *The Hedge Knight*, *The Sworn Sword* and *The Mystery Knight* (recently published in the *Warriors* anthology (March 2010)). The stories relate the adventures of **Dunk** (eponymously called Ser Duncan the Tall, a legendary member of the Kingsguard before the time of A Song of Ice and Fire) and **Egg** (the later King Aegon V in a disguised role), beginning with their meeting eighty-nine years before the events of the main cycle and intended to cover a long period of time. Martin has indicated there will be several more stories, as many as nine, covering much of the life stories of the two protagonists.

The Hedge Knight

The Hedge Knight	
Graphic Novel (Second edition)	
Author	George R. R. Martin
Country	United States
Language	English
Series	A Song of Ice and Fire
Genre(s)	Fantasy
Publisher	Dabel Brothers Productions
Publication date	March 25, 2005
Media type	Original novella in Legends anthology; released as standalone graphic novel
Pages	160
ISBN	ISBN 097640110X (graphic novel)
OCLC Number	57692652 [1]
Followed by	*The Sworn Sword*

The first novella was originally published August 25, 1998 in the *Legends* anthology, edited by Robert Silverberg. The story was later adapted to a six issue comic book limited series by Ben Avery, drawn by Mike S. Miller, produced by Roaring Studios (now Dabel Brothers Productions) and published by Image Comics and Devil's Due between August 2003 and May 2004. Devil's Due published the complete limited series as a graphic novel in June 2004, following the termination of the partnership between Dabel Brothers and Devil's Due, the graphic novel has been republished in various editions.

A hedge knight, Ser Arlan of Pennytree, has died during the night. His squire, a large young man named Dunk, buries him and pays his last respects. After considering several options, Dunk decides to continue his journey to Ashford and compete in the tourney as a knight. He adopts Ser Arlan's armor as his own, as well as his equipment, three horses, and remaining monies. At an inn on the road, he meets a boy with a shaved head named Egg, who offers to become his squire. Despite the fact that Dunk, calling himself Ser Duncan the Tall, declines the offer, Egg secretly follows him to Ashford. Impressed by the boy's spirit, Dunk takes him on as his own squire for the upcoming tourney.

At Ashford, Dunk sells one of his horses so he can commission a suit of armor by the smith Pate. He also befriends Ser Steffon Fossoway's squire and cousin, Raymun Fossoway. Without proof of his knighthood, however, he is nearly barred from competition until Prince Baelor Targaryen vouches for him. Baelor tells Dunk that as he is not of Ser Arlan's family, he cannot use his arms, so Dunk commissions a Dornish puppeteer girl to paint a new one. Dunk watches the first day of competition amongst the commoners, with Egg on his shoulders. After several spectacular tilts, the day ends after Prince Aerion Targaryen disgraces himself by killing Ser Humphrey Hardyng's horse.

That night, when Dunk retires into the Fossoways' tent to drink with Raymun, Egg informs that a puppeteer girl he had met earlier is being beaten by Prince Aerion. Dunk leaps to her defense and attacks Aerion, striking him in the face. As the royal guard arrests Dunk, Egg reveals himself to be Aerion's brother, Prince Aegon. Imprisoned, Dunk is visited by Egg, who tells that he was meant to be Prince Daeron's, his older brother's, squire. Being a poor warrior, Daeron stole away from the escort, leading Aegon to pose as Egg in order to fulfill his dream of being a squire. After meeting Prince Baelor again, Dunk chooses to take a trial by combat rather than undergo mutilation (the removal of the offending hand and foot which he used to assault a royal prince). Prince Aerion demands the combat to be a Trial of Seven, as his brother, Prince Daeron, the drunkard from the inn, had also accused Dunk of kidnapping Aegon from his charge. The council of lords, including Lord Ashford, Baelor and Aerion's father, Maekar, have no choice but to accept the demand. Dunk must find six champions to fight with him against seven accusing knights, or he must forfeit.

Steffon Fossoway is the first ally Dunk finds. He promises to bring Dunk more champions, as does Raymun. Egg also promises to bring more champions for Dunk's cause. Prince Daeron, also called the Drunken, appears in the tent. He confesses Egg's earlier accusations, and that he fabricated his own charges at the trial as he was embarrassed of losing track of his brother while in drunken stupor. He warns Dunk that his father will have three knights of the Kingsguard fight in the trial. He also tells

Dunk of an ominous dream where he saw Dunk with a dead dragon, the symbol of House Targaryen, and assures that his dreams always come true.

Dunk is met again by Pate, who was trusted by the puppeteer girl with Dunk's new shield. At the morning of the trial, Raymun returns with Ser Humfrey Hardyng and Ser Humpfrey Beesbury, good-brothers seeking revenge for the grievance Aerion committed against Hardyng. Aegon brings Ser Robyn Rhysling and Ser Lyonel Baratheon (called the "Laughing Storm"), both eager for the glory of competing in the first Trial of Seven in a century. Steffon returns only to say he has decided to fight with the accusers for the reward of a lordship. Angered by his cousin's treachery, Raymun begs to be knighted and fight in Steffon's place. Dunk hesitates, as the truth to his own knighthood is questionable, and knighting Raymun would also jeopardize his future as well. Dunk is called away by Lord Ashford, and Lyonel grants Raymun his knighthood. Still needing a seventh champion, Dunk appeals unsuccessfully to the crowd. Finally, Prince Baelor announces that he will champion Dunk himself, though the accusers include three of his family members.

The fourteen champions line their mounts along opposite sides of the tourney grounds and charge. Dunk tilts against Aerion, but is quickly unhorsed. Though nearly defeated, Dunk manages to grapple Aerion and use his size advantage and streetfighting style to pummel Aerion into submission with his own shield. Aerion recants his accusation, ending the Trial. The fighting costs the lives of both Humphreys. After the battle, Baelor approaches Dunk to congratulate him, and begins to act drunkenly. When his crushed helm is removed, it is shown that the weaker armor made for his son did not protect him from a blow which has crushed in his skull, fulfilling Daeron's prophetic dream. Prince Maekar meets with Dunk after the funeral, revealing that it was his mace that killed Baelor. He regrets Aerion's behavior and offers Dunk a position in his household to train Aegon. Dunk insists on being allowed to travel, and offers to take Aegon as his squire to learn to be a better knight than Aerion. Maekar agrees, making sure Aegon continues to use his alias of Egg to avoid scandal. Dunk and Egg set out to Dorne, in search of the puppeteer whom Dunk had saved.

The Sworn Sword

The second novella was published 2003 in the *Legends II* anthology, also edited by Robert Silverberg. The story has been adapted to a graphic novel by Ben Avery and drawn by Mike S. Miller, in cooperation with publisher and distributor Marvel Comics. The graphic novel is due out in 2008 with the first comic released on June 20, 2007 [2].

Dunk and Egg travelled Dorne in search of the puppeteer Dunk had saved at Ashford, but never found her. A great plague called the Spring Sickness passed during their stay in Dorne. During a great drought, they left the hedges to enter regular service of a master. The story begins in the Reach with Dunk sworn to Ser Eustace Osgrey of Standfast, an old and broken man whose family were once lords of Coldmoat. Dunk and Egg's adventure illuminates several aspects of the feudal system of Westeros. Also, a series of flashbacks narrated by Ser Eustace relate the events of the Blackfyre Rebellion and its conclusion at the Battle of the Redgrass Field of 196 AL.

Loaded with supplies, Dunk and Egg journey back to the fort of Standfast. Upon their return, Dunk and Ser Eustace's other sworn sword, Ser Bennis the Brown, go to investigate the local stream, which has dried up. They discover that a dam has been built by peasants in service to Lady Rohanne Webber of Coldmoat. Bennis cuts one of the peasants and scares them all away. Upon hearing the news, Ser Eustace realizes that Lady Webber, known as the "Red Widow" for both her sigil of the spider and her red hair, will be angered by Bennis's actions. He orders Dunk and Bennis begin training levies from his three villages.

Hoping for a peaceful solution, Eustace sends Dunk to Coldmoat to discuss the matters of the dam and the wounded servant. Upon entering Coldmoat, Dunk learns that Lady Rohanne is widowed and stands to lose her lands if she does not take a husband soon. Her castellan, the haughty Ser Lucas Inchfield (known as the Long Inch for his height, 6-foot 7-inches), is her most aggressive suitor. Dunk meets with Rohanne, and the two experience a subtle sexual tension. However, Dunk is unable to change her mind on either the dam's construction or seeking justice for her servant. In return, Rohanne informs him that Ser Eustace is a former traitor, having supported the usurper Daemon Blackfyre.

Shocked by the news, Dunk returns to Standfast to leave Ser Eustace's service. That night, Ser Eustace's forest is put to the torch. Lady Rohanne had informed Dunk after their failed negotiations that if Ser Bennis were not sent to her to suffer her judgment, she would bring "fire and sword" to Ser Eustace. The burning of Wat's Wood has fulfilled the fire portion of that claim, so Dunk fears that Rohanne will bring her knights in the early morning and slaughter Eustace's levies, which number only seven men. He disperses the levies, enraging Eustace. Dunk placates him by promising to stand by him and face the Lady together.

At the river, they meet the Lady and her thirty-plus knights, including Ser Lucas Long Inch. Ser Eustace reminds Dunk of the method whereby his ancestor the Little Lion had saved the Reach from an attack by Lannisters by killing the leader of the attackers. By doing so, he hopes that Dunk will kill Lady Rohanne and remove her threat to him and avenge past slights. Instead, Dunk offers his own blood to Lady Rohanne by slicing his own cheek. This pays the debt of the cut peasant, but in claiming that Lady Rohanne had Wat's Wood burned, Ser Eustace has slighted her honor. She requires apology or vindication, as she personally claims innocence of the matter.

All parties agree to settle the matter through trial by combat between Dunk and Ser Lucas. They fight in the river as it is the only neutral ground present. Dunk is nearly outfought by Ser Lucas, but uses his grappling skills to drown the other knight. He drowns in the process but is resuscitated by Lady Rohanne's maester, who was ironborn and knows the ways of the Drowned God.

Severely wounded and barely alive, Dunk is taken to Coldmoat to be tended by the maester for his injuries. When he awakens, Dunk learns that Ser Eustace and Lady Rohanne have reconciled and become married. Before Dunk leaves, Rohanne offers him her finest mare to make amends. He refuses, claiming that he is unworthy of such a horse, and a horse is not what he would have of her. Lady

Rohanne insists that he take something to remember her by, so he kisses her passionately. Egg meets Dunk shortly after, and wonders what happened to the horse Lady Rohanne promised to give Dunk. Dunk informs him that he didn't want the horse, but that as a token to remember her, he cut her long braid and will keep it. Dunk and Egg then set off to continue their travels.

The Mystery Knight

The third novella was published in 2010 in the anthology *Warriors*. Warriors was edited by George R. R. Martin and Gardner Dozois.

Like *The Sworn Sword*, the book takes place during the reign of Aerys I and the aftermath of the Blackfyre Rebellion is examined in more detail.

The story begins with Dunk and Egg leaving Stoney Sept. They are moving north to try and take up service with Lord Beron Stark who has sent a call for men to help fend off Greyjoy raids on the northern coast. On the way they encounter a septon who was beheaded for preaching treason; Dunk remembers that Lord Bloodraven has spies everywhere. On route Egg and Dunk encounter a lord's train led by Lord Gorman Peake of Starpike, whose arms are three black castles on a field of orange. Also in the party are a lord named Alyn Cockshaw and a well dressed and richly garbed man who claims to be a hedge knight named Ser John the Fiddler. Dunk is challenged and insulted by Peake and Cockshaw but the Fiddler treats him courteously. Before they ride off, Ser John invites Dunk to attend the wedding of Lord Ambrose Butterwell. There is to be a joust to celebrate the wedding of Butterwell to a Frey of the Crossing, the victor's prize is to be a dragon egg.

Dunk takes a dislike to Gorman Peake; Ser Arlan to whom Dunk was squired claimed his previous squire Roger of Pennytree was slain by Gorman in the battle of Redgrass field. Egg tells Dunk that Peake's arms of three castles on an orange field is because the Peake family used to own three castles, but two were forfeited to the Crown when Peake sided with Blackfyre.

Dunk decides to go to the wedding. During the journey Dunk befriends three fellow hedge knights, Ser Maynard Plumm, Ser Kyle the Cat of Misty Moor and a young hedge knight named Ser Glendon Ball who claims he is the bastard son of the famous knight Quentyn "Fireball" Ball, a renowned warrior who fought for Daemon Blackfyre.

The wedding is set at Whitewalls and Lord Frey arrives with his four year old heir (Walder Frey) and his fifteen year old daughter, who weds Lord Butterwell. Egg tells Duncan that Lord Butterwell took no part in the Blackfyre Rebellion, but one of his sons fought for the Red Dragon and one for the Black. In that way his house was guaranteed to be on the winning side, but both his sons died on the Redgrass field. Egg becomes increasingly suspicious at the wedding and points out to Duncan that many of the banners and sigils he sees are of men who fought for the Black Dragon. Dunk tells Egg that Redgrass was over a decade ago, and the past is the past. At the wedding a troupe of dwarfs entertain the guests. During the bedding Dunk is drafted by John the Fiddler to carry the bride to the bedchamber. Dunk does so and later when he goes for a breath of air, John the Fiddler talks to him saying that he recognized Dunk on the road. Dunk appeared to him in a dream in which Duncan wore the all white armour of the Kingsguard. The Fiddler says his dreams always come true, as he dreamt his brothers dead once and also a dragon hatching from an egg at Whitewalls.

Dunk decides to enter the first match of the joust as a mystery knight known as the Gallows Knight (due to a new shield that once belonged to a knight of House Trant that Dunk had to buy as his old shield was damaged in his duel with Longinch) in case anyone heard of a Knight named Ser Duncan the Tall from Ashford, but Dunk is defeated in the first tilt by Ser Uthor Underleaf known as the Snail Knight due to his sigil. Underleaf's lance hits Duncan upon the helm, knocking him out and nearly killing him. Dunk recovers later and goes to give the Underleaf his armour and horse as forfeit (losing a joust match requires a forfeit of horse and armour to the winner). Since Dunk can't ransom it back he is in a glum mood. Dunk talks to Underleaf and Underleaf informs Dunk that someone bribed him to try and kill Dunk in the final tilt, Underleaf states that if they paid more he might have completed the task, but tells Dunk he has an enemy. Before the jousting continues word spreads through the castle that the dragon egg is missing and the blame is placed on Ser Glendon Ball, who is imprisoned by Peake.

Dunk notices that Egg is missing and sets out to find his squire. Whilst searching he is almost killed by Alyn Cockshaw who tells Dunk he bribed Underleaf to kill Dunk because he was jealous of John the Fiddler's obsession with Dunk and that dream (it is implied that Cockshaw was in love with John the Fiddler) Dunk manages to defeat him by throwing him down a well, though he takes a wound in return from Cockshaws knife. Maynard Plumm comes to Duncan's aid , and it is discovered that Plumm is one of Bloodravens many spies, and that John the Fiddler's real name is Daemon, after his father Daemon Blackfyre. Plumm tells Dunk "he would be suprised how many Lords want their king to be brave and stupid".

Dunk finds Egg in the sept with the cowering Lord Butterwell, who on discovering Egg's true identity is terrified for his life. Egg told Ambrose (falsely) that he and Dunk were spies sent to investigate the tournament and that his father Maekar is on the way with an army. Lord Ambrose good son (stepson) Black Tom Heddle shows up and tries to harm Egg but is slain by Dunk. Dunk tells Egg to flee with Ambrose. To buy time for Egg's escape Dunk confronts Daemon Blackfyre, accusing Gorman Peake of falsely charging Ball with the theft of the dragon egg.

Daemon is enraged by the implication and allows Ball to prove his innocence in trial by combat. Ser Glendon soundly defeats Daemon and knocks him into the mud causing some of the spectators to mockingly call Daemon *"the Brown Dragon"*. By this time a large army under the King's Hand Brynden Rivers encircles Whitewalls and Daemon is captured as most of the present Lords and knights surrender without a fight. Dunk meets Bloodraven inside his pavilion outside of which the head of Gorman Peake along with Black Tom Heddle are displayed on spears. Egg is there as well and demands that Bloodraven reward Ser Glendon Ball, Dunk and all the other hedge knights. Bloodraven notes that Egg is much more fierce and confident now and that he was the dragon Daemon saw in his dream being born at Whitewalls. Lord Butterwall cowers in Bloodraven's presence and is allowed to keep a tenth of his wealth. Whitewalls, however, will be forfeit to the Iron Throne and torn down. Bloodraven, in gratitude to Dunk, gives him the gold to ransom his armour back. Dunk then asks Bloodraven what became of the dragon egg. Bloodraven tells Dunk it was taken by an agent of his who crawled up the privy shaft of the castle to take the egg from its guarded chamber, and is now safe. Dunk remarks that a man wouldn't have fit in those shafts. Bloodraven replies a child would have. Or a dwarf, Dunk thinks as he remembers the performing dwarfs at the wedding.

House Targaryen at the time of the Hedge Knight (208)

	Rhaenyra							
Aegon III		Viserys II						
Daena		Aegon IV		Naerys	Aemon the Dragonknight			
Daemon Blackfyre	Aegor "Bittersteel" Rivers	Brynden "Bloodraven" Rivers	Shiera Seastar	Myriah Martell	Daeron II	Daenerys		
Aegon Blackfyre	Aemon Blackfyre	Baelor Breakspear	Aerys	Aelinor	Rhaegal	Maekar		
	Valarr	Matarys	Daeron	Aerion	Aemon	Aegon	Rhae	Daella

See also: House Targaryen.

References in other Song of Ice and Fire Novels

Ser Duncan the Tall is listed among notable Commanders of the Kingsguard when Jaime Lannister is self-reflecting in *A Storm of Swords*. In the same chapter it is mentioned in the recordings of Barristan Selmy that he defeated Ser Duncan the Tall in the winter tourney of King's Landing.

From the genealogy chart of Targaryens in the reference section of *A Game of Thrones*, it shows that Egg would become King Aegon V (the Unlikely) and rule from 233-259. This was confirmed in *A Clash of Kings*, where it is revealed that Egg's brother Maester Aemon was offered the throne, he refused and suggested that Egg rule instead. As king, Egg wanted Aemon to help him rule, but Aemon chose to continue his maestering work and went to the Wall instead.

In *A Feast for Crows*, Brienne has her shield painted with arms that match Dunk's. Brienne takes the arms from a shield she remembers seeing in her father's armory. Also in a *A Feast for Crows* Brienne arrives at an inn owned by a girl whose last name is Heddle (possible descendant of Black Tom Heddle who is killed by Dunk in the Mystery Knight).

Also in *A Feast for Crows*, Maester Aemon mentions Egg's name several times in his delirium. It is revealed that one of Egg's daughters married a son of House Baratheon and became the mother of Lord Steffon Baratheon, and thus the grandmother of Robert, Renly and Stannis Baratheon.

External links

- A Wiki Of Ice And Fire [2] Wiki dedicated to A Song of Ice and Fire
- *Tales of Dunk and Egg* [3] at the Internet Book List

Adaption for TV

Game of Thrones (TV series)

Game of Thrones	
Title screen as seen in the first teaser	
Genre	Medieval fantasy
Format	Serial drama
Created by	**Series:** David Benioff Dan Weiss **Novels:** George R. R. Martin
Written by	David Benioff Dan Weiss Bryan Cogman Jane Espenson George R. R. Martin
Directed by	Thomas McCarthy Brian Kirk Daniel Minahan Alan Taylor Timothy Van Patten

Starring	Mark Addy Alfie Allen Sean Bean Emilia Clarke Nikolaj Coster-Waldau Peter Dinklage Michelle Fairley Aidan Gillen Jack Gleeson Iain Glen Kit Harington Lena Headey Isaac Hempstead-Wright Harry Lloyd Richard Madden Rory McCann Sophie Turner Maisie Williams
Country of origin	United States
Language(s)	English
No. of seasons	1
No. of episodes	10 (0 aired)
Production	
Executive producer(s)	David Benioff Dan Weiss co-executive producers: Carolyn Strauss Guymon Cassady Vincent Gerardis Ralph Vicinanza George R. R. Martin
Producer(s)	Mark Huffam Frank Doelger
Location(s)	Northern Ireland Malta
Cinematography	Marco Pontecorvo Alik Sakharov
Broadcast	
Original channel	HBO

Picture format	1080i (HDTV)
Status	In production
External links	
Official website [1]	

Game of Thrones is an upcoming American medieval fantasy television series created by David Benioff and Dan Weiss for HBO. The series, based on author George R. R. Martin's best-selling *A Song of Ice and Fire* series of novels, chronicles the violent dynastic struggles among noble families for control of the Iron Throne of Westeros. HBO programming chief Michael Lombardo has stated that the series will likely debut in Spring 2011.

Production

Conception and development

The series began development in January 2007, when HBO, after acquiring the rights for *A Song of Ice and Fire* with the intent of turning the novels into a television series, hired David Benioff and Dan Weiss to write and executive produce the series, which would cover one novel's worth of material per season. Initially, it was planned that Benioff and Weiss would write every episode save one, which author and co-executive producer George R. R. Martin was attached to write, of every season, but Jane Espenson and Bryan Cogman were later added to respectively pen one episode of the first season.

"*The Sopranos* in Middle-earth" is the tagline Benioff jokingly suggested for the television adaptation, referring to its intrigue-filled content and dark tone set in a fantasy setting. Fantasy is described to be incidental to the series, with magic taking a back seat to storytelling, which is what HBO programming chief Michael Lombardo found appealing in spite of the network's new developmental policy to "[take] shots at shows that we wouldn't have taken a shot at five years ago." Nonetheless, HBO hired expert language creator David J. Peterson from the Language Creation Society to develop a Dothraki language — "possessing its own unique sound, extensive vocabulary of more than 1,800 words and complex grammatical structure" — to be used in the series. The first and second drafts of the pilot script, written by Benioff and Weiss, were submitted in August 2007 and June 2008, respectively. While HBO found both drafts to their liking, a pilot was not ordered until November 2008, with the 2007–2008 Writers Guild of America strike possibly delaying the process.

Although *Game of Thrones*'s budget has been compared to that of *Rome,* the project appeared to be more expensive than it actually was, its first shooting of the pilot reportedly costing HBO between US$5 to $10 million. *Game of Thrones* is set to premiere on screen sometime during Spring 2011.

Casting

On May 5, 2009, it was announced that Peter Dinklage had been signed on to star as Tyrion Lannister in the pilot, and that Tom McCarthy was set to direct. Shortly thereafter, pranksters at the Internet Movie Database edited the IMDb profile [2] of actress Holly Marie Combs to indicate that she had been cast as Catelyn Stark; however, producers David Benioff and Dan Weiss confirmed that this was a hoax. A few months later, in the beginning of August, it was revealed that Catelyn would be portrayed by Jennifer Ehle.

In the late hours of July 19, 2009, a number of further casting decisions were announced, including Sean Bean being given the role of Ned Stark, thus confirming a rumour first reported a couple of days before. Other actors signed on for the pilot were Kit Harington in the role of Jon Snow, Jack Gleeson as Joffrey Baratheon, Harry Lloyd as Viserys Targaryen, and Mark Addy as Robert Baratheon.

On August 20, several more casting announcements were made, featuring Nikolaj Coster-Waldau as Jaime Lannister and Tamzin Merchant as Daenerys Targaryen, as well as Richard Madden in the role of Robb Stark, Iain Glen as Ser Jorah Mormont, Alfie Allen as Theon Greyjoy, and the young Sophie Turner and Maisie Williams as Sansa and Arya Stark, respectively. On September 1, it was revealed that Lena Headey had been cast as Cersei Lannister. On September 23, Martin confirmed that Rory McCann has been cast as Sandor Clegane. Isaac Hempstead-Wright was confirmed as Bran Stark on October 14, followed by an announcement of Jason Momoa as Khal Drogo three days later.

After the pilot was shot and the series picked up, it was announced that the role of Catelyn had been recast, with Michelle Fairley replacing Ehle. Later, it was also confirmed that Emilia Clarke would replace Tamzin Merchant as Daenerys.

Filming locations

Principal photography for the first season of the series was scheduled to begin on July 26, 2010, with the primary locations being Paint Hall Studio in Belfast, Northern Ireland, and Malta, a change in location from Morocco. For the initial shooting of the pilot in 2009, additional filming locations included Carncastle, Shane's Castle, Castle Ward, Magheramorne Tollymore Forest Park in Northern Ireland, and Doune Castle in Scotland.

Cast and characters

For a more comprehensive list, see List of characters in Game of Thrones

- Mark Addy as King Robert Baratheon
- Alfie Allen as Theon Greyjoy
- Sean Bean as Eddard "Ned" Stark
- Emilia Clarke as Daenerys Targaryen
- Nikolaj Coster-Waldau as Ser Jaime Lannister
- Peter Dinklage as Tyrion Lannister
- Michelle Fairley as Catelyn Stark
- Aidan Gillen as Petyr "Littlefinger" Baelish
- Jack Gleeson as Joffrey Baratheon
- Iain Glen as Ser Jorah Mormont
- Kit Harington as Jon Snow
- Lena Headey as Cersei Lannister
- Isaac Hempstead-Wright as Bran Stark
- Harry Lloyd as Viserys Targaryen
- Richard Madden as Robb Stark
- Rory McCann as Sandor "The Hound" Clegane
- Sophie Turner as Sansa Stark
- Maisie Williams as Arya Stark

Plot

Main article: Synopsis of A Song of Ice and Fire

The television series is expected to follow the multiple storylines of the *A Song of Ice and Fire* series of novels closely, and author Martin has stated that the pilot script was very faithful to his work. Set in Westeros where "summers span decades and winters can last a lifetime," *Game of Thrones* chronicles the violent dynastic struggles among noble families for control of the Iron Throne.

Reception

Anticipation for the series has been described by various media outlets as extremely high, with a dedicated fan base closely following the show's early development.

Notes and references

External links

- Official website [1]
- George R. R. Martin's Official Website [3]
- *Game of Thrones* [2] at the Internet Movie Database
- *Game of Thrones* [3] at TV.com

Character Lists

List of characters in A Song of Ice and Fire

List of characters in *A Song of Ice and Fire*, George R. R. Martin's fantasy book series and its fictional universe. More information for notable characters can be found on Major houses in A Song of Ice and Fire and Characters in A Song of Ice and Fire, depending on whether the character belongs to Major house or not.

:	A B C D E F G H I J K L M N O P Q R S T U V W X Y Z

A

- Abelar Hightower, challenger at the Ashford tourney.
- Addam Marbrand, a knight in the service of House Lannister. Heir to Ashemark. Became Lord Commander of The City Watch of King's Landing and friend to Jaime Lannister.
- Addam Osgrey, son of Eustace Osgrey, slain on the Redgrass Field during the Blackfyre Rebellion.
- Aegon Blackfyre, son of Daemon Blackfyre, killed at the Redgrass Field during the Blackfyre Rebellion.
- Aegon Frey, called Jinglebell. A halfwit fool at the Twins, killed by Catelyn Stark.
- Aegon Frey, eldest son of ser Aenys Frey. Outlaw of the riverlands.
- Aegon I Targaryen, called the Conqueror. First King of the Seven Kingdoms.
- Aegon II Targaryen, killed in the Dance of Dragons.
- Aegon III Targaryen, called the Dragonslayer and Dragonsbane.
- Aegon IV Targaryen, called the Unworthy
- Aegon V Targaryen, called Egg and the Unlikely
- Aegon Targaryen, infant son of Rhaegar. Killed during the sack of King's Landing.
- Aegor Rivers, called "Bittersteel". A legitimized bastard of Aegon IV and rebel to the throne.
- Aelinor Targaryen, queen to Aerys I.
- Aemon Blackfyre, son of Daemon Blackfyre, killed at the Redgrass Field during the Blackfyre Rebellion.
- Aemon Costanye, a singer.
- Aemon Estermont, eldest son and heir to Lord Eldon Estermont, loyal to King Joffrey.
- Aemon Rivers, son of "Bastard" Walder Rivers of house Frey.
- Aemon Targaryen, called the Dragonknight and member of the Kingsguard.

- Aemon Targaryen, a maester in the Night's Watch.
- Aenys Frey, a knight, third son of Lord Walder Frey.
- Aenys I Targaryen, Aegon the Conqueror's son.
- Aerion Targaryen, called Brightflame.
- Aeron Greyjoy, called Damphair, eighth son of Lord Quellon Greyjoy, and a priest of the Drowned God.
- Aerys I Targaryen, second son of King Daeron II, succeeded by his younger brother Maekar.
- Aerys II Targaryen, last Targaryen King, also known as "the Mad King".
- Aethan
- Grand Maester Aethulmure, long dead.
- Aggar
- Aggo, A member of Daenerys's *khas*, and later her bloodrider.
- Aladale Wynch, knight of the Night's Watch, dead at the Battle of the Skull Bridge.
- Alan
- Alaric
- Alayaya, daughter of Chataya and whore in her upscale King's Landing brothel.
- Albar Royce, a knight and heir to the Gates of the Moon.
- Albett, a new-member of the Night's Watch.
- Alebelly, a Winterfell guard.
- Alekyne Florent, Only son of Lord Alester Florent.
- Alerie Tyrell, daughter of Lord Leyton Hightower and wife to Lord Mace Tyrell. Mother of Willas, Garlan, Loras and Margaery Tyrell.
- Alesander Frey, a singer who was sent away from the Twins before the Red Wedding because he was loyal to the Northsmen.
- Alesander Staedmon, Lord of Broad Arch, called the Pennylover.
- Alester Florent, Lord of House Florent, Hand of the King to Stannis Baratheon, burned at the stake for treason.
- Alfyn, a wildling leader.
- Alia of Braavos, a singer at King Joffrey's wedding.
- Alla Tyrell, daughter of ser Leo Tyrell and far cousin to Margaery.
- Allar Deem, a brutal captain of the King's Landing City Watch.
- Allard Seaworth, second son of Ser Davos Seaworth.
- Alliser Thorne, knight. Brother of The Night's Watch and master-at-arms of Castle Black.
- Allyria Dayne, sister to Ser Arthur Dayne and to Ashara Dayne. Betrothed to Lord Beric Dondarrion.
- Alyce
- Alyce Graceford, Lady of Godsgrace.

- Alyn, a Winterfell guard. He led the Stark host against ser Gregor Clegane at the Battle of Mummer's Ford.
- Alyn Ambrose, a squire, betrothed to Alla Tyrell.
- Alyn Estermont, a knight, son of ser Aemon Estermont, loyal to King Joffrey.
- Alyn Stackspear, a knight of the Westerlands. He seems to be the real father of the baby of the Harrenhal jailer's wife.
- Alys Karstark, only daughter of Lord Rickard Karstark.
- Alysanne Bulwer, lady of Blackcrown.
- Alysanne Targaryen, sister and wife to King Jaehaerys I Targaryen.
- Alyssa Arryn, long-ago Lady of House Arryn, mythical namesake of the waterfall Alyssa's Tears
- Alys Frey, wife and cousin to ser Jared Frey. She is long dead.
- Alyx Frey
- Amabel
- Ambrode
- Amerei Frey, known as "Gatehouse Ami," deserted wife of Lancel Lannister.
- Amory Lorch, a landed knight and vile bannerman of House Lannister.
- Andar Royce, a knight and heir to Runestone.
- Anders Yronwood, foster father of Prince Quentyn Martell. He is titled Warden of the Boneway and The Bloodroyal.
- Andrew Estermont, a knight, son of Ser Lomas Estermont, loyal to King Stannis.
- Andrey Charlton, a knight sworn to House Frey, killed by Lannisters.
- Andrey Dalt, close companion of Princess Arianne Martell and heir to Lemonwood.
- Andrik, called "the Unsmiling". A powerful raider of the Iron Islands.
- Andros Brax, Lord of Hornvale, killed during the Battle of the Camps.
- Androw Ashford, a knight at the Ashford tourney, oldest son of Lord Ashford.
- Anguy, called "the Archer". A skilled archer of the Brotherhood without Banners who won the archers challenge during the Hand of the King's tourney.
- Antario Jast, a lord sworn to House Lannister, captured by Stark forces at the Battle of Oxcross.
- Anya Waynwood, Lady of Ironoaks Castle, keeps Harold Hardyng as her ward.
- Ardrian Celtigar, Lord of Claw Isle.
- Areo Hotah, Captain of the guard at Sunspear, hails from the free city of Norvos
- Argilac, called "the Arrogant". The last Storm King.
- Arlan of Pennytree, a hedge knight, master of Dunk.
- Arneld
- Arnell, a knight of the Night's Watch; his mother was a Fossoway.
- Aron Santagar, master-at-arms of the Red Keep.
- Arrec, the Storm King who lost the riverlands to the ironborn led by Harwyn Hoare.

- Arron Qorgyle, a knight, second son of Lord Quentin Qorgyle and companion of Prince Oberyn Martell at King's Landing.
- Arryk, a famous member of the Kingsguard who slew and was slain by his brother Erryk during the Dance of Dragons.
- Arryk, called either "Left" or "Right". One of Olenna Redwyne's bodyguards.
- Arson
- Arthur Ambrose, Lord of Ambrose and sworn to House Tarly.
- Arthur Dayne, called "Sword of the Morning". A hero of the Kingsguard. Slain at the Tower of Joy.
- Artos Stark
- Arwyn Frey, first daughter of Lady Annara Farring and Lord Walder Frey.
- Arwyn Oakheart, Lady of Old Oak.
- Arya Stark, daughter Lord Eddard Stark, also called Underfoot, Cat of the Canals, and Arry, among others. POV character.
- Arymidon
- Arys Oakheart, member of the Kingsguard and younger son of Lady Arwyn Oakheart.
- Asha Greyjoy, daughter of Lord Balon Greyjoy.
- Ashara Dayne, sister to ser Arthur Dayne. She killed herself when she gained knowledge of the death of her brother by Lord Eddard Stark. Some say she is the real mother of Jon Snow.
- Lord Ashford, arranged the Ashford tourney.
- Aubrey Ambrose, supporter of Daemon Blackfyre.
- Aurane Waters, called "The Bastard of Driftmark". A sellsail that was promoted to Master of Ships for the kingdom. Absconded with the entire fleet.
- Azor Ahai, legendary hero of the R'hllor faith.

B

- Bael, called "Bael the Bard"
- Baelor I Targaryen, called "Baelor the Blessed" or "Baelor the Beloved".
- Baelor Targaryen, called "Breakspear". Present at the Ashford tourney
- Ball, called "Fireball"
- Ballabar, maester of the Arbor.
- Balon Greyjoy, Lord Reaver of Pyke
- Balon Swann, a very skilled knight, younger son of Lord Gulian Swann.
- Bandy
- Bannen, a skilled ranger of the Night's Watch.
- Barra, a bastard of King Robert I
- Barre, a septon.

- Barristan Selmy, called "the Bold". Lord Commander of the Kingsguard under both Aerys II Targaryen and Robert Baratheon. Dismissed following Robert Baratheon's death and now in service with Daenerys Targaryen.
- Barth
- Barth Stark
- Bass
- Beardless Dick
- Becca
- Bedwyck, called "Giant". A diminutive ranger of the Night's Watch.
- Belis, a pyromancer.
- Bella, claims to be a bastard of King Robert I
- Belwas, called "Strong Belwas". A eunuch and former pit-fighter, now one of Daenerys's Queensguards.
- Ben
- Ben Blackthumb, old blacksmith of Harrenhal.
- Ser Benedict Broom, master-at-arms at Casterly Rock.
- Benfred Tallhart, eldest son of ser Helman Tallhart and heir to Torrhen's Square. He is the leader of a knight company, known as the "Wild Hares".
- Benfrey Frey, a knight, twentieth son of Lord Walder Frey and husband to Jyanna Frey, his cousin.
- Benjen Stark, a man of the Night's Watch and First Ranger of Castle Black. Lost beyond the Wall for well over a year.
- Bennis of the Brown Shield, hedge knight in the service of Eustace Osgrey.
- Beren Tallhart, second son of Leobald Tallhart.
- Berena Tallhart, sister of Lord Halys Hornwood and wife to Leobald Tallhart.
- Beric Dondarrion, Lord of Blackhaven.
- Bernarr
- Beron Stark
- Bessa
- Beth Cassel, daughter of Rodrik Cassel.
- Bethany
- Bethany Frey, sixth wife to Lord Walder Frey, she is a Rosby by birth.
- Bethany Rowan, wife to Lord Mathis Rowan, a Redwyne by birth.
- Big Boil
- Bill
- Biter, a cannibal and prisoner in the black cells of King's Landing.
- Blane, a member of the Night's Watch.
- Bluetooth, a longship captain.
- Bodger

- Bonifer Hasty, called "the Good". The pious leader of the "Holy Hundred".
- Borcas
- Boros Blount, a knight of the Kingsguard, known to be a coward
- Bowen Marsh, First Steward of The Night's Watch.
- Brandon Stark
- Brandon Stark. Eldest son of Lord Rickard Stark and older brother of Ned. Murdered by Aerys Targaryen
- Brandon Stark, son of Lord Eddard, simply called "Bran".
- Bran the Builder, legendary figure who built the Wall.
- Brenett
- Brienne of Tarth, only living daughter of Lord Selwyn Tarth.
- Bronn, a dangerous mercenary known to be exceptionally shrewd and agile. Previously served as captain of Tyrion Lannister's personal guard.
- Bryan Fossoway, a member of the House Fossoway of Cider Hall (Red Apple).
- Bryce Caron, Lord of Nightsong and of the Marches. The Orange of King Renly's Rainbow Guard.
- Bryen Caron, long dead Lord of Nightsong and of the Marches, father to Lord Bryce Caron and to Ser Rolland Storm.
- Bryen Farring, royal squire of King Stannis.
- Byren Flowers, called "Black Byren". Supporter of Daemon Blackfyre.
- Brynden Rivers, Lord Bloodraven. Bastard son of Aegon IV.
- Brynden Tully, called "the Blackfish", younger brother to Lord Hoster Tully.
- Burton Crakehall, a knight, younger brother to Lord Roland Crakehall.
- Butterbumps, fat fool of the Tyrell household.
- Butterwell
- Buu
- Lord Butterwell, Hand of Daeron II.
- Byan Votyris

C

- Cadwyl
- Cadwyn
- Lord Cafferen
- Calon, a Winterfell boy, Cayn's son.
- Carellen Smallwood, daughter of Lord Theomar Smallwood.
- Cass
- Cassana Baratheon of House Estermont, wife to Lord Steffon Baratheon and mother of King Robert, Lord Stannis and Lord Renly.

- Lord Caswell, Lord of Bitterbridge.
- Catelyn Stark, a daughter of House Tully and wife to Eddard Stark.
- Cayn, a Winterfell guard.
- Cellador, a septon and brother of the Night's Watch.
- Cerrick, maester at Coldmoat.
- Cersei Baratheon
- Cersei Frey, called "Little Bee", daughter of ser Raymund Frey.
- Chataya, mistress of an upscale brothel in King's Landing.
- Chayle, septon of Winterfell.
- Chella
- Chelsted
- Chett, a steward of the Night's Watch.
- Chiggen, a mercenary.
- Chiswyck, a soldier under Ser Gregor Clegane's command.
- Clement Piper, Lord of Pinkmaiden.
- Cleon, a slave of Grazdan Mo Ullhor, also a butcher and cook.
- Cleos Frey, a knight, eldest son of ser Emmon Frey and cousin to Lannisters.
- Cley Cerwyn, heir to Cerwyn.
- Ser Cleyton Caswell, suitor of Rohanne Webber.
- Clifford Conklyn, claimant to Lady Webber's Leafy Lake.
- Clydas, steward of the Night's Watch.
- Coldhands, a mysterious figure from beyond the Wall that can control ravens.
- Colemon, maester of the Eyre.
- Cohollo, the oldest Khal Drogo's bloodrider.
- Colen of Greenpools, a hedge knight at the service of Lord Renly Baratheon.
- Ser Colin Florent, brother to Alester Florent.
- Collio Quaynis
- Conn
- Conwy, a recruiter of the Night's Watch.
- Cortnay Penrose, a knight and castellan of Storm's End.
- Cotter Pyke, Lord Commander of Eastwatch-by-the-Sea.
- Craster, a brutal wildling friend of the Night's Watch.
- Crawn
- Cregan Stark, a renowned warrior who once fought the Dragonknight.
- Maester Cressen, old maester at Dragonstone.
- Cuger, a new member of the Night's Watch.
- Cutjack

D

- Daario Naharis, the captain of the Stormcrows.
- Dacey Mormont, a warrioress and heiress of Bear Island.
- Daella Targaryen, daughter of Baelor "Breakspear."
- Daemon Blackfyre, a Targaryen great-bastard legitimized, leader of the Blackfyre Rebellion.
- Daemon Sand, a knight, called "The Bastard of Godsgrace"
- Daena Targaryen, sister and wife of Baelor I Targaryen (marriage dissolved), mother of Daemon Blackfyre. She was called "the Defiant".
- Daenerys Targaryen, the last known family member of House Targaryen
- Daeron I Targaryen, called the "Young Dragon"
- Daeron II Targaryen, called the Good.
- Daeron Targaryen, eldest son of Maekar. Also known as "the Drunk".
- Daeryssa Targaryen, Princess saved by Serwyn of the Mirror Shield.
- Dafyn Vance, a knight of the riverlands.
- Dagmer, called "Dagmer Cleftjaw" and "the Cleftjaw". An infamous raider of the Ironmen.
- Dagos Manwoody, Lord of Kingsgrave.
- Dalbridge, a veteran ranger of the Night's Watch.
- Dale Seaworth, eldest son of ser Davos Seaworth and his heir.
- Dalla
- Damon Vypren, a knight and heir to Lord Lucias Vypern.
- Dan, called Hempen Dan. A wildling raider.
- Dancy, a whore at Chataya's brothel.
- Danos Slynt, son of Janos Slynt.
- Danwell Frey, a knight, tenth son of Lord Walder Frey and husband to Lady Wynafrei Whent.
- Dareon, an apprentice singer forcibly put into the Night's Watch.
- Daryn Hornwood, heir to Hornwood.
- Daven Lannister, a valiant knight, son of ser Stafford Lannister.
- Davos Seaworth, the "Onion Knight". A landed knight loyal to King Stannis Baratheon, and master of Cape Wrath.
- Del, a wildling raider.
- Delp, a guard of Riverrun.
- Dennet, a knight of the Brotherhood without Banners.
- Denys Arryn, "the Darling of the Vale", a knight, heir to his cousin Lord Jon, dead at the Battle of Stoney Sept.
- Denys Mallister, an old and valorous knight, Lord Commander of the Shadow Tower.
- Dermont of the Rainwood, a knight.
- Desmond, a guard of Winterfell.
- Desmond Grell, a knight and master-at-arms of Riverrun.

- Devan Seaworth, a royal squire of King Stannis.
- Dezial Dalt, the Knight of Lemonwood.
- Dickon Manwoody, second son of Lord Dagos Manwoody.
- Dickon Tarly, son of Lord Randyll Tarly and heir of Horn Hill.
- Dirk, a member of the Night's Watch.
- Dobber
- Domeric Bolton, dead son and heir of Lord Roose Bolton and heir.
- Donal Noye, one-armed blacksmith of the Night's Watch at Castle Black, formerly of Storm's End.
- Donella Hornwood, Lady of Hornwood.
- Donnel Haigh, knight of the riverlands, at the service of House Frey.
- Donnel Hill, called "Sweet Donnell Hill" of the Night's Watch.
- Donnel Locke, a knight, heir of Oldcastle.
- Donnel Waynwood, knight of the Bloody Gate and second son of Lady Anya Waynwood.
- Donnel of Duskendale, a knight in Daeron II Targaryen's Kingsguard.
- Donnis
- Donnor Stark
- Dontos Hollard, called "the Red". A drunkard knight, the last of his House.
- Doran Martell, Lord of Sunspear and Prince of Dorne.
- Dorcas, a handmaiden of Cersei Lannister.
- Dorea Sand, seventh of the Sand Snakes, illegitimate daughter of Oberyn Martell and Ellaria Sand.
- Doreah, a handmaiden of Daenerys Targaryen and former pleasure slave.
- Dormund, one of many Tormund Giantsbane's sons.
- Dorren Stark
- Drennan
- Drogo, an undefeated Dothraki *khal*.
- Dryn, a son of Tormund Giants-bane.
- Dudley
- Dunaver, a knight at Harrenhal in Tywin's service.
- Dunk, called "Ser Duncan the Tall". The Hedge Knight. Later Lord Commander of the Kingsguard.
- Dunsen, called "Shitmouth". A soldier under Gregor Clegane.
- Duram Bar Emmon, Lord of Sharp Point.
- Durran, called "Durran Godsgrief". The semi-legendary first Storm King.
- Lord William Dustin, killed fighting the Kingsguard at the Tower of Joy.
- Dyah
- Dykk Harlaw, an Ironborn raider placed under Theon's authority.
- Dywen, a veteran ranger of the Night's Watch.

E

- Ebben, one of Qhorin's rangers in the Night's Watch.
- Eddard Karstark, third Son of Rickard Karstark.
- Eddard Stark, Lord of Winterfell and Lord Protector of the North.
- Edderion Stark
- Eddison Tollett, a squire of the Night's Watch, called "Dolorous Edd".
- Edmure Tully, a knight, only son and heir of Lord Hoster Tully.
- Edmyn Tully, first Lord Tully of Riverrun.
- Edric Dayne, the young Lord of Starfall, squire to Lord Beric Dondarrion.
- Edric Storm, a bastard of Robert Baratheon and Delena Florent, fostered at Dragonstone.
- Edrick Stark
- Edwyd Fossoway, a knight of the House Fossoway of Cider Hall (Red Apple).
- Edwyle Stark, long dead Lord of Winterfell, father of Lord Rickard and grandfather of Lord Eddard.
- Edwyn Frey, son of ser Ryman Frey and husband to Janyce Hunter.
- Edwyn Osgrey, son of Eustace Osgrey, slain on the Redgrass Field.
- Edwyn Stark
- Eggon a soldier under Ser Gregor Clegane.
- Egon Emeros
- Elbert Arryn, Jon Arryn's nephew, killed by King Aerys II Targaryen.
- Eldiss
- Eldon Estermont, the old Lord of Greenstone Castle.
- Elenya Westerling, daughter of Lord Gawen Westerling.
- Elia Targaryen, sister to Prince Doran Martell and dead wife of Prince Rhaegar Targaryen.
- Elia Sand, fifth of the Sand Snakes, illegitimate daughter of Oberyn Martell and Ellaria Sand.
- Elinor Tyrell, daughter of ser Theodore Tyrell and betrothed to Alyn Ambrose. Cousin to Margaery.
- Ellaria Sand, paramour of House Martell#Oberyn Martell and mother of the four youngest Sand Snakes. Bastard daughter of Lord Harman Uller.
- Elmar Frey, twenty-eighth son of Lord Walder Frey. Betrothed to Arya Stark when Robb passes the Crossing.
- Elwood
- Elwood Meadows, Lord of Grassy Vale and lieutenant of the Storm's End castellan Ser Cortnay Penrose.
- Elyas Willum, Lord Willum's second son.
- Elys Westerling, a knight of House Westerling during the War of the Usurper.
- Emmon Cuy, a knight called "the Yellow". One of Renly's Rainbow Guard.
- Emmon Frey, second son of Lord Walder Frey, husband to Genna Lannister.
- Endehar, an Ironborn raider placed under Theon's authority.
- Endrew Tarth, a knight of the Night's Watch.

- Enger
- Eon Hunter, old Lord of Longbow Hall.
- Ermesande Hayford, the infant Lady of Hayford.
- Eroeh, a Lhazareeni.
- Erryk, a famous member of the Kingsguard who slew and was slain by his brother Arryk during the Dance of Dragons.
- Erryk, called either "Left" or "Right". One of Olenna Redwyne's bodyguards.
- Erreg
- Erren Florent, a knight, son of ser Ryam Florent.
- Errok
- Erryk
- Esgrid
- Ethan Glover, former squire to Brandon Stark.
- Euron Greyjoy, called "Crow's Eye", fifth son of Lord Quellon Greyjoy. Chosen by his people as the Lord of the Iron Islands following the death of his older brother Balon Greyjoy.
- Eustace Osgrey. Landed knight in Sworn Sword. Ser Duncan the Tall served him for a time. Fought for Daemon Blackfyre during the Blackfyre Rebellion.
- Eyron Stark

F

- Falyse Byrch, heiress of Stokeworth and wife to ser Balman Byrch.
- Farlen, kennelmaster of Winterfell.
- Lord Farman of Fair Isle, raided by Dagon Greyjoy's Ironmen.
- Lord Fell of Fellwood
- Fern
- Ferny
- Flement Brax, a knight of the westerlands, third son of Lord Andros Brax.
- Fletchwood Dick, the most skilled archer of the Brotherhood of Kingswood.
- Fogo
- Forley Prester, a knight, cousin to Lord Garrison Prester of Feastfires.
- Fornio
- Frenken, master of Stokeworth.

G

- Gage, head cook at Winterfell.
- Galbart Glover, Master of Deepwood Motte, Lord Robett's younger brother.
- Gallard, an Archmaester of the Citadel.
- Galt, a Stone Crow.
- Galyeon of Cuy, a singer.
- Gared, an earless veteran ranger of the Night's Watch.
- Gareth Clifton, a knight and husband to Lady Jeyne Farman.
- Gareth "the Grey."
- Garigus, a pyromancer.
- Garin, an orphan of the Greenblood and old friend of Princess Arianne Martell.
- Gariss, a guard of Winterfell.
- Garlan Tyrell, called "the Gallant", knight and second son of Lord Mace Tyrell.
- Garth of Greenaway, a ranger of the Night's Watch.
- Garth "Greenhand", legendary first king of the Reach.
- Garth "Greyfeather" a ranger of the Night's Watch.
- Garth Hightower, a knight and fourth son of Lord Leyton Hightower.
- Garth of Oldtown, a ranger of the Night's Watch.
- Garth Tyrell, called "the Gross", uncle to Lord Mace Tyrell.
- Gascoyne of the Greenblood, a knight and sworn shield to Prince Trystane Martell.
- Gawen Westerling, Lord of the Crag.
- Gawen Wylde, formerly master-at-arms of Storm's End during the War of the Usurper.
- Gelmarr "the Grim," an ironborn raider in Theon's crew.
- Gendel
- Gendry, apprentice blacksmith and bastard son of Robert Baratheon.
- Genna Frey, wife to ser Emmon Frey and sister to Lord Tywin Lannister.
- Gerald Gower, a knight at the service of King Stannis Baratheon.
- Gerald Grafton, Lord of Gulltown.
- Gerardys, long dead Grand Maester.
- Gerold Dayne, nicknamed "Darkstar". Part of the plot to place Myrcella Baratheon on the throne, tried to kill her when it failed.
- Gerion Lannister, youngest son of Lord Tytos Lannister. Dead in the search for Brightroar, the ancient Valyrian steel sword of House Lannister.
- Gerold Hightower, called "The White Bull". Lord Commander of the Kingsguard.
- Gerren
- Gevin Harlaw, member of House Harlaw and of Theon's crew.
- Ghost of High Heart, an old sage.
- Gilbert Farring, a knight loyal to Stannis.

- Gilly, a Wildling girl.
- Gladden Wylde, a knight of Rainhouse, sent by Lord Eddard Stark fighting against ser Gregor Clegane.
- Goady
- Godwyn
- Lord Goodbrook of Goodbrook
- Gormon
- Gormon Peake. A supporter of Daemon Blackfyre.
- Gorne
- Gowen Baratheon
- Lord Grandison of Grandview.
- Grazdan, founder of the ancient Ghiscari empire.
- Grazdan mo Eroz, an envoy and nobleman.
- Grazdan mo Ullhor, a rich slave trader.
- Greenbeard, a member of the Brotherhood without Banners. His true name is Pello of Tyrosh.
- Gregor Clegane
- Grenn, a ranger of the Night's Watch.
- Grey King, legendary first king of the Isles.
- Grey Worm, captain of Daenerys's Unsullied.
- Grigg the Goat, a Wildling raider.
- Groleo, captain of Saduleon.
- Grubbs, a ranger of the Night's Watch.
- Gueren, a recruiter of the Night's Watch.
- Gulian, a maester.
- Gulian Qorgyle
- Gulian Swann, Lord of Stone Helm and father of ser Donnel and ser Balon Swann.
- Guncer Sunglass, Lord of Sweetport Sound.
- Guthor Grimm, Lord of Greenshield.
- Guyard Morrigen, a knight, the Green of the Rainbowguard.
- Gwayne Corbray, Kingsguard of Daeron II.
- Gylbert Farwynd, Lord of the Lonely Light.
- Gyles Farwynd, heir of the Lonely Light.
- Gyles Grafton, son of Lord Gerold Grafton and his heir.
- Gyles Rosby, Lord of Rosby
- Gynir

H

- Haggo, Khal Drogo's bloodrider.
- Hake, a steward of the Night's Watch.
- Hal
- Halder, a new member of the Night's Watch.
- Hali
- Hallis Mollen, commander of the Guard of Winterfell after Jory Cassel.
- Hallyne, a pyromancer and Wisdom of the Guild of Alchemists in King's Landing.
- Halys Hornwood, Lord of Hornwood.
- Hamish
- Ser Harald Osgrey, son of Eustace Osgrey, slain on the Redgrass Field.
- Harbert Baratheon, old uncle to Lord Steffon Baratheon and castellan at Storm's End.
- Hareth
- Harlan Grandison, knight of Aerys's Kingsguard, replaced by ser Jaime Lannister.
- Harlen Tyrell
- Harma, called "Dog's Bane"
- Harmen Uller, Lord of Hellholt. Father of Ellaria Sand, Oberyn Martell's paramour and mother of the youngest of the Sand Snakes.
- Harra
- Harrag Harlaw, also known as "Sheepstealer", a member of Prince Theon Greyjoy's crew.
- Harren Hoare, known as "Black Harren", the builder of Harrenhal.
- Harrion Karstark, eldest son and heir of Lord Rickard Karstark.
- Harwin, a Winterfell guard, later a member of the Brotherhood Without Banners.
- Harwyn Hoare, grandfather to Harren Hoare, he conquered the riverlands by defeating the Storm King, Arrec.
- Harys Swyft, Hand of King Tommen. "Good-father" (father-in-law) of Kevan Lannister via Kevan's marriage to Harys' daughter Dorna.
- Hayhead
- Helicent Uffering, Roland Uffering's sister, at Coldmoat.
- Helly
- Helman Tallhart, the Knight of Torrhen's Square.
- Helya
- Hendry Bracken, a knight, nephew and heir to Lord Jonos Bracken.
- Henk the Helm, a wildling raider.
- Heward
- Hibald, a fearful and niggardly merchant.
- Hobb, "Three Fingers", cook of the Night's Watch.
- Hobber Redwyne, called "Slobber". A knight. Son of Lord Paxter Redwyne, twin to Horas.

- Hod
- Hodor, a giant, lackwit stableboy at Winterfell. His true name is Walder.
- Horas Redwyne, called "Horror". A knight. Son of Lord Paxter Redwyne, twin to Hobber.
- Hosteen Frey, a knight of House Frey.
- Hoster Tully, Lord of Riverrun.
- Hot Pie, friend to Arya Stark
- Hother Umber, called "Whoresbane". An uncle to the Greatjon.
- Howland Reed, Lord of Greywater's Watch and old friend to Lord Eddard Stark. Possibly the only living character who knows the truth of Jon Snow's parentage.
- Hubard Rambton, a knight of the Crownlands.
- Hugh
- Hullen, Harwin's father.
- Humphrey Beesbury, a knight in The Sworn Sword.
- Humphrey Hardyng, a knight in The Sworn Sword.
- Husband, owner of the Inn near the Ruby Ford.

I

- Iggo, a Brave Companion.
- Igon Vyrwel, Captain of the Guards at Highgarden.
- Illyrio Mopatis, a magister of the Free City of Pentos.
- Ilyn Payne, a knight and King's Justice, the royal executioner.
- Imry Florent, a knight, son of ser Ryam Florent.
- Ironbelly
- Irri, a handmaiden of Daenerys Targaryen.

J

- Jacelyn Bywater, called "Ironhand", a knight. Succeeded Janos Slynt as Lord Commander of the City Watch in King's Landing. Killed by his own men during King Stannis' attack on King's Landing.
- Jack
- Jacks, a Winterfell guard.
- Jaehaerys I Targaryen
- Jaehaerys II Targaryen
- Jafer Flowers, a ranger of Night's Watch.
- Jaggot
- Jaime Lannister, called "the Kingslayer", a knight and current Lord Commander of the Kingsguard under King Tommen. Had his right hand cut off by Vargo Hoat.

- Jalabhar Xho, exiled prince of the Red Flower Vale on the Summer Islands.
- Jammos Frey
- Janna Fossoway
- Janos Slynt, Lord Commander of the City Watch in King's Landing until Tyrion Lannister, as Hand of the King, sent him to the Wall.
- Jaqen H'ghar
- Jared Frey
- Jaremy Rykker, second ranger of the Night's Watch.
- Jarl
- Jarmen Buckwell, ranger of the Night's Watch.
- Jason Mallister, Lord of House Seaguard. Famed warrior during the War of the Usurper, Greyjoy's Rebellion and the War of the Five Kings.
- Jate
- Jeffory Mallister, companion of Brandon Stark, executed by King Aerys.
- Jeor Mormont, the "Old Bear", Lord Commander of the Night's Watch. Murdered by his own men at Craster's Keep beyond the Wall.
- Jeren, a new member of the Night's Watch.
- Jeyne Poole, Vayon Poole's daughter and a friend to Sansa Stark.
- Jeyne Targaryen
- Jeyne Westerling, wife of Robb Stark.
- Jhaqo, a Dothraki khal.
- Jhiqui, a handmaiden of Daenerys Targaryen.
- Jhogo, Daenerys' bloodrider.
- Joanna Lannister, late wife of Tywin Lannister
- Jodge
- Joffrey Baratheon, eldest son of King Robert Baratheon and heir to the Iron Throne.
- Jojen Reed, son of Howland Reed, Lord of Greywater's Watch.
- Jommo
- Jommy
- Jon Arryn
- Jon Connington, Hand of the King under Aerys II.
- Jon Fossoway, a knight of House Fossoway of New Barrel (Green Apple).
- Jon Snow, bastard son of Lord Eddard Stark. 998th Lord Commander of the Night's Watch.
- Jon Umber, called the Greatjon. Lord of the Last Hearth.
- Jon Umber, called the Smalljon. Heir to the Last Hearth.
- Jonnel Stark
- Jonos Bracken, Lord of Stone Hedge.
- Jonos Stark

- Jonothor Darry, knight of Aerys' Kingsguard, brother to ser Willem Darry.
- Jorah Mormont, son of Jeor Mormont, knight in exile, once Lord of Bear Island.
- Jorah Stark
- Joramun
- Jorgen, a peasant of Coldmoat.
- Jory Cassel, Captain of the Guard at Winterfell, nephew of ser Rodrik Cassel.
- Joseth
- Josmyn Peckledon, a squire.
- Joss
- Joss Stilwood, squire to Ser Gregor Clegane.
- Josua Willum, Lord Willum's eldest son.
- Jothos Slynt
- Joy Hill, bastard daughter of Gerion Lannister.
- Joyeuse Frey
- Jyck
- Jynessa Blackmont
- Jyzene

K

- Karl
- Karlon Stark
- Karyl Vance, Lord of Wayfarer's Rest.
- Kedge
- Kenned
- Kennos of Kayce, often sounds the Horn of Herrock
- Ketter
- Kevan Lannister
- Khorane Sathmantes
- Knight of Ninestars, slain by Daemon Blackfyre on the Redgrass Field.
- Koss
- Kraznys mo Nakloz
- Kromm
- Kurleket, a Bracken man-at-arms who accompanies Catelyn and Tyrion through the Mounatains of the Moon.
- Kurz
- Kyle
- Kyle Condon

- Kyle Royce
- Kym
- Kyra

L

- Lamprey, gaoler at Dragonstone.
- Lancel V Lannister, a King of the Rock, killed by Wilbert Osgrey
- Lancel Lannister, son of Kevan Lannister. A squire to King Robert Baratheon.
- Lann the Clever, a legendary trickster.
- Lanna
- Larence Snow, called "the Bastard of Hornwood".
- Lark
- Larra Blackmont
- Layna
- Left Hand Lucas Codd
- Lem, called "Lemoncloak". A member of the Brotherhood Without Banners.
- Lenn
- Lenyl
- Leo Lefford, Lord of Goldentooth.
- Leobald Tallhart, castellan of Torrhen's Square.
- Leonette Tyrell
- Leslyn
- Leslyn Haigh
- Lestor Morrigen, Lord of Crow's Nest.
- Lew Piper, a squire to Ser Jaime Lannister.
- Lewyn Martell, member of the Kingsguard
- Lewys Lydden
- Leyton Hightower, voice of Oldtown, Lord of the Port, Lord of the High Tower, Defender of the Citadel and Beacon of the South.
- Lharys
- Lollys Stokeworth.
- Lommy Greenhands, a boy on his way to join the Night's Watch.
- Loras Tyrell, Knight of the Kingsguard. Last reported to have been maimed by boiling oil during the siege of Dragonstone, and dying.
- Loren I Lannister, last King of the Rock, knelt to Aegon I the Dragon.
- Loreza Sand, eighth of the Sand Snakes. Illegitimate daughter of Oberyn Martell and Ellaria Sand.
- Lorren, called "Black Lorren". An infamous ironborn raider.

- Lothar Frey
- Lothar Mallery
- Lothor Brune, a freerider.
- Lucas Blackwood, heir to Raiventree.
- Ser Lucas Inchfield, called "The Longinch."
- Lucas Roote
- Lucius Vypren
- Luke
- Luthor Tyrell
- Luwin, maester at Winterfell
- Lyanna Mormont, the youngest of Maege Mormont's daughters. Named after Lyanna Stark.
- Lyanna Stark
- Lyel Crakehall, called the "Strongboar". Famed knight and battle commander.
- Lyessa Flint, Lady of Widow's Watch.
- Lyle Crakehall
- Lyman Darry
- Lymond Goodbrook
- Lymond Lychester
- Lymond Vikery
- Lyn Corbray, master swordsman and suitor to Lysa.
- Lync
- Lynesse Mormont, *nee* Hightower, estranged second wife of Ser Jorah.
- Ser Lyonel Baratheon, called "The Laughing Storm." A famous knight who attended the Ashford tourney.
- Lysa Tully Arryn
- Lythene Vypren

M

- Mace Tyrell
- Mad Huntsman, a brutal member of the Brotherhood without Banners and castellan of Stony Sept.
- Maege Mormont, Lady of Bear Island.
- Maegor I Targaryen, called the Cruel.
- Mag Mar Tun Doh Weg, called "Mag the Mighty", King of the giants
- Malcolm
- Mallador Locke
- Malleon
- Malliard

- Mallor
- Mance Rayder, The King beyond the Wall
- Mandon Moore
- Mandred Lothson, Lord of Harrenhal.
- Manfred Dondarrion, Lord of House Dondarrion during The Hedge Knight. Refused to vouch for Ser Duncan the Tall for his entry into the Ashford Tournament.
- Marei
- Margaery Tyrell
- Marianne Vance
- Maric Seaworth
- Marillion, a singer
- Marissa Frey
- Mariya Frey
- Mark Mullendore
- Mark Ryswell
- Maron Botley
- Maron Greyjoy
- Marq Piper, heir to Pinkmaiden.
- Martyn Cassel
- Martyn Lannister
- Martyn Rivers
- Marwyn, an Archmaester of the Citadel.
- Marya Seaworth, a cobbler's daughter before her marriage to Lord Davos.
- Masha Heddle
- Maslyn
- Matarys Targaryen
- Mathis Rowan, Lord of Goldengrove.
- Mathos Mallarawan
- Matrice
- Matthar
- Matthos Seaworth, son of Davos Seaworth
- Mawney
- Maynard, a Septon.
- Mebble
- Medger Cerwyn
- Meera Reed, daughter of Howland Reed
- Megga Tyrell
- Meizo Mahr

- Melisandre of Asshai, called "The Red Woman". A priestess of R'hllor in the service of Stannis Baratheon
- Melessa Florent, daughter of Alester Florent, wife of Randyll Tarly
- Melly
- Meredyth Crane
- Merianne Frey
- Meribald, a wandering septon.
- Merlon Crakehall
- Mern IX Gardener
- Mero
- Merrett Frey
- Merrit
- Merryweather
- Meryn Trant
- Mikken, blacksmith of Winterfell.
- Minsa Tully
- Mirri Maz Duur, a *maegi*, or witch-woman
- Missandei
- Mohor
- Monford Velaryon
- Monterys Velaryon
- Moon Boy, a fool at King's Landing.
- Mord, a gaoler in the Eyrie
- Mordane, a septa at Winterfell
- Moreo Tumitis
- Morgil, called "the Evil"
- Moro
- Morosh the Myrman
- Morrec
- Morros Slynt
- Mors Manwoody
- Mors Martell
- Mors Umber
- Morton Waynwood
- Moryn Tyrell
- Mudge
- Mullin
- Munciter

- Munda
- Murch
- Murmison
- Mya Stone, bastard daughter of Robert Baratheon
- Mycah, a butcher's boy at Winterfell
- Mychel Redfort
- Myles
- Myles Manwoody
- Myles Mooton, squire to Prince Rhaegar Targaryen, later killed by Robert Baratheon at the Stoney Sept.
- Myles Smallwood
- Myrcella Baratheon
- Myranda Royce, daughter of Nestor Royce
- Myria Jordayne
- Myriah Targaryen

N

- Naerys Targaryen
- Nage
- Nan, called "Old Nan". Longtime servant at Winterfell.
- Nella
- Nestor Royce, High Steward of the Vale
- Nissa Nissa
- Notch
- Nute the Barber
- Nymeria
- Nymeria Sand, second of the Sand Snakes, illegitimate daughter of Oberyn Martell. Also known as Lady Nym.
- Nysterica

O

- Obara Sand, eldest of the Sand Snakes, illegitimate daughter of Oberyn Martell
- Obella Sand, sixth of the Sand Snakes, daughter of Oberyn Martell and Ellaria Sand.
- Oberyn Martell
- Ogo
- Olenna Tyrell, known as the "Queen of Thorns".
- Ollo Lophand
- Olyvar Frey, squire of King Robb Stark.
- Omer, a Maester of The Citadel, in service at Old Oak. Son of Ser Colin Florent.
- Omer Blackberry, one of Stannis Baratheon's sworn swords.
- Ondrew Locke
- Orell, called "the Eagle", a wildling skinchanger.
- Ormond
- Ormond Osgrey
- Orphan Oss
- Orton Merryweather, a Tyrell bannerman and husband of Taena Merryweather.
- Orys Baratheon
- Osfryd Kettleblack, a sellsword and brother to Osmund and Osney.
- Osha, wildling warrior captured by Robb Stark. Entrusted to keep Rickon Stark safe following the sack of Winterfell.
- Osmund Kettleblack, a sellsword knight and brother to Osfryd and Osney.
- Osmynd
- Osney Kettleblack, a sellsword and brother to Osfryd and Osmund.
- Oswell Kettleblack, a sellsword and father of Ser Osmund, Osfryd and Osney.
- Oswell Whent
- Oswyn
- Othell Yarwyck
- Otho Bracken, called "the Brute of Bracken". Killed Lord Blackwood at a tourney at King's Landing.
- Othor
- Otter Gimpknee
- Otto Hightower
- Ottyn Wythers
- Owen Norrey

P

- Palla
- Parmen Crane, the Purple knight of the Rainbowguard.
- Patchface, lackwit fool at Dragonstone
- Pate, a novice at the Citadel
- Pate of the Blue Fork
- Pate, Prince Tommen's whipping boy.
- Patrek Mallister, heir to Seagard.
- Paul
- Paxter Redwyne, Lord of the Arbor.
- Penrose
- Perros Blackmont
- Perwyn Frey, a knight.
- Perwyn Osgrey, called "the Proud". Founder of House Osgrey.
- Petyr Baelish
- Petyr Frey, called "Petyr Pimple"
- Phillip Foote, a knight.
- Pia, called "Pretty Pia".
- Podrick Payne, a timid squire of a lesser branch of House Payne
- Pollitor
- Polliver, captain of Gregor Clegane's men.
- Pono
- Porridge, a gaoler at Dragonstone
- Porther
- Poul Pemford
- Poxy Tym, a guardsman at Winterfell.
- Praed
- Prendahl na Ghezn, a former captain of the Stormcrows.
- Preston Greenfield
- Puddingfoot
- Pyat Pree, one of Qarth's warlocks.
- Pycelle, the Grand Maester
- Pyg, a member of the Brave Companions
- Pylos, the Maester of Dragonstone.
- Pypar, a man of Night's Watch.

Q

- Qalen
- Qarl, an Ironborn raider
- Qhorin, called "Halfhand", an experienced ranger of the Night's Watch
- Qorgyle
- Qos
- Qotho
- Quaithe of the Shadow, a shadowbinder from Asshai
- Quaro
- Quent
- Quenten Banefort
- Quhuru Mo
- Quickfinger, a failed assassin during the Blackfyre Rebellion
- Quort
- Qyburn, a Maester stripped of his chain. A member of the Brave Companions. Replaced the eunuch Varys as Lord of Whispers in King's Landing. Currently sits on King Tommen's Small Council.
- Qyle

R

- Rafford, called "Raff the Sweetling" or "Raff". A soldier under Ser Gregor Clegane
- Ragwyle, a wildling spearwife
- Rakharo, bloodrider to Daenerys Targaryen
- Ramsay Snow, called "The Bastard of Bolton"
- Randyll Tarly, Lord of House Tarly and a Tyrell bannerman
- Rast
- Rattleshirt, the self-styled "Lord o' Bones"
- Ravella Smallwood
- Raymar Royce
- Raymun
- Raymun Darry
- Raymund Frey
- Raynald Westerling
- Redtusk
- Redwyn
- Reek, a repellent companion to Ramsay Snow
- Regenard Estred
- Renly Baratheon, King in Highgarden.

- Reynard Webber, Lord of House Webber
- Reysen
- Rhaelle Targaryen, sister to Aegon V
- Rhaegar Targaryen
- Rhaella Targaryen
- Rhaenys Targaryen
- Rhaenys Targaryen
- Rhea Florent, Daughter of Alester Florent, wife of Leyton Hightower
- Rhogoro
- Richard Lonmouth
- Rickard Karstark, Lord of Karhold and a Stark bannerman
- Rickard Stark, father of Eddard Stark
- Rickon Stark youngest son of Catelyn & Eddard Stark
- Robar Royce
- Robb Reyne
- Robb Stark, eldest son of Lord Eddard and Lady Catelyn Stark. Proclaimed King in the North. Betrayed and murdered at the Twins by Lord Walder Frey.
- Robert Arryn
- Robert Baratheon
- Robett Glover
- Robin Flint, was an escort for Lady Catelyn Stark. Killed at the Red Wedding.
- Robin Ryger, Captain-of-the-guard at Riverrun and friend to Hoster and Edmure Tully.
- Rodrik Cassel, a knight and Master-at-arms of Winterfell
- Rodrik Stark
- Rodwell Stark
- Roland Crakehall, a knight of King Daeron II's kingsguard.
- Ser Roland Uffering, Lady Rohanne Webber's fourth husband, died in the Great Spring Sickness.
- Rolfe
- Rollam Westerling
- Rolland Storm
- Rolley
- Rolph Spicer
- Ronel Rivers
- Ronnel Harclay
- Ronnel Stout
- Ronnet "Red Ronnet" Connington, right hand man of Jaime Lannister during the siege of Riverrun.
- Roone
- Roose Bolton

- Rorge, noseless prisoner of the black cells at King's Landing
- Roslin Frey
- Rossart
- Rupert Brax
- Ryam Florent
- Ryam Redwyne, historic Lord Commander of the Kingsguard.
- Ryger Rivers
- Ryk
- Ryles
- Ryman Frey
- Rymund
- Ryon Allyrion

S

- Salladhor Saan, a Lyseni pirate.
- Sallei Frey
- Sallor the Bald, former captain of the Stormcrows.
- Salloreon
- Sam Stoops, the steward of Steadfast.
- Samwell Tarly, morbidly obese man of the Night's Watch. Sometimes called "Sam the Slayer" or "Lord Piggy". Well-meaning and learned, but notoriously craven.
- Sandor Clegane, known throughout Westeros as "The Hound". Member of the Kingsguard, last seen by Arya Stark when he was gravely wounded. Clegane wears a dog's-head helm and has severe burns to one side of his face inflicted by his older brother Gregor when the two were young boys.
- Sansa Stark
- Sarella Sand, fourth of the Sand Snakes, illegitimate daughter of Oberyn Martell.
- Sarra Frey
- Satin, soldier of the Night's Watch
- Sawane Botley, Lord of Lordsport on Pyke.
- Sawwood
- Sefton, a septon.
- Selwyn Tarth, called the Evenstar, Lord of Tarth.
- Selyse Baratheon, of House Florent, wife of Stannis Baratheon. Queen.
- Serra Frey
- Serwyn of the Mirror Shield, a legendary Kingsguard knight.
- Shadd
- Ser Shadrick of the Shady Glen, a hedge knight in Hibald's service.

- Shae, 18-year-old whore in the service of Tyrion Lannister during his tenure as King Joffrey's Hand.
- Shagga, son of Dolf. A leader of the Stone Crows clan from the Mountains of the Moon.
- Shagwell, called "the Fool". A member of the Brave Companions mercenary company
- Sharna, innkeep at the Inn of the Kneeling Man.
- Shella Whent, formerly Lady of Harrenhal.
- Shiera "Seastar", one of the Great Bastards of King Aegon IV. Frequent paramour of Lord Bloodraven.
- Shireen Baratheon, young daughter of Stannis Baratheon has been deformed by the greyscale disease.
- Shirei Frey
- Shitmouth, a soldier in the garrison at Harrenhal. Known for his obscene language.
- Shyra
- Shyra Errol
- Sigrin, a Lordsport shipwright.
- "Silveraxe" Fell, Lord of Fellwood.
- Ser Simon Leygood, suitor of Rohanne Webber.
- Ser Simon Staunton, Lady Rohanne Webber's third husband, choked upon a chicken bone.
- Simon Toyne, an infamous outlaw of the Kingswood Brotherhood. Killed by Ser Barristan the Bold.
- Skittrick
- Skyte
- The Smiling Knight, an infamous outlaw of the Kingswood Brotherhood. Killed by Ser Arthur Dayne.
- Softfoot
- Squint
- Squinty Jeyne, a peasant on Osgrey lands, mother of half-wit Rob.
- Lord Stackhouse, covets Lady Webber's Horseshoe Hills.
- Stafford Lannister
- Stannis Baratheon
- Stannis Seaworth, son of Davos Seaworth.
- Steffon Baratheon
- Steffon Seaworth, son of Davos Seaworth.
- Steffon Varner
- Stevron Frey
- Stiv
- Stone Thumbs
- Stonesnake, a member of the Night's Watch.
- Stygg
- Styr, called "the Magnar of Thenn". Leader of the Thenn, a tribe of wildlings beyond the North.

- Sumner Crakehall
- Sybelle Westerling
- Sybelle Glover
- Sylas
- Sylva Santagar, close companion of Princess Arianne Martell.
- Symeon Star Eyes, legendary hero.
- Symon, called Silvertongue. A singer.
- Symond Frey
- Syrio Forel, former First Sword of Braavos.

T

- Taena Merryweather, Myrish beauty. Wife of Orton Merryweather and Lady of the House. Confidante and pillow-friend to Queen Cersei.
- Talla Tarly
- Tallad
- Tanda Stokeworth, Lady of House Stokeworth.
- Tanselle, a puppeteer accosted by Aerion Brightflame and rescued by Ser Duncan the Tall. Dornish.
- Tansy
- Tanton Fossoway
- Tarber
- Temmo
- Theo Wull
- Theomar Smallwood, Lord of Acorn Hall.
- Theon Greyjoy, only living son of Balon Greyjoy and heir to the Iron Islands. Raised as a ward of Eddard Stark after Balon Greyjoy's rebellion against Robert Baratheon. Betrayed Robb Stark and sacked Winterfell. Currently a prisoner of Roose Bolton's bastard son Ramsay Snow.
- Theon Stark
- Thoren Smallwood
- Thoros, called "Thoros of Myr". A red priest of R'hllor in King's Landing.
- Three Toes, a Brave Companion.
- The Tickler, a soldier and expert torturer serving Gregor Clegane.
- Tim Stone, a ranger and Sworn Brother of the Night's Watch.
- Tim Tangletongue, a steward at Castle Black.
- Timeon of Dorne, a Brave Companion.
- Timett
- Timett, son of Timmett. Leader of the Burned Men clan of the Mountains of the Moon.
- Ser Timon Scrapesword, a famed knight.

- Tion Frey, son of Emmon Frey and Genna Lannister.
- Tobbot
- Tobho Mott, a master armorer in King's Landing.
- Todder
- Todric
- Toefinger
- Togg Joth, a Brave Companion. Originally from Ibben.
- Tom of Sevenstreems, a singer. Also called Tom O'Sevens.
- TomToo, son of Tomard
- Tomard, called "Fat Tom". A guardsman at King's Landing.
- Tommen Baratheon
- Toregg
- Tormund, known as "Giant's Bane" among other titles.
- Torrek
- Torrhen Karstark
- Torrhen Stark
- Tothmure
- Tregar
- Tregar Ormollen
- Tremond Gargarlen
- Tristifer IV Mudd
- Tristifer V Mudd
- Tristimun
- Trystane Martell, youngest child of Prince Doran Martell.
- Tuffleberry
- Tumberjon
- Turnip
- Turquin
- Tya Baratheon
- Tyene Sand, third of the Sand Snakes, illegitimate daughter of Oberyn Martell
- Tygett Lannister
- Tymor
- Tyrek Lannister
- Tyrion Lannister, called "The Imp". Served as King Joffrey's Hand for a time before being deposed by his father, Tywin Lannister. Falsely accused of murdering King Joffrey, Tyrion was freed from prison by his brother Jaime and has fled Westeros.
- Tysha, Tyrion Lannister's first wife
- Tyta Frey

- Tytos Blackwood, Lord of House Blackwood. Follower of the Old Gods and one of the few remaining commanders still in the field after the War of the Five Kings.
- Tytos Brax
- Tytos Lannister
- Tywin Lannister father of Jaime, Cersei, and Tyrion Lannister. Lord of Casterly Rock and Warden of the West under King Robert. Later assumes the role of Hand under King Joffrey. Murdered in his own privy at King's Landing by his son Tyrion.

U

- Ulf of the Moon Brothers
- Ulf the Ill, an Ironborn raider placed under Theon's authority.
- Uller
- Ulmer
- Ulrick Dayne, a past Sword of the Morning.
- Ulwyck Uller
- Urreg
- Urron Greyiron
- Urswyck, called "Faithful Urswyck". A member of the Brave Companions mercenary company.
- Urzen
- Utherydes Wayn, steward of Riverrun and House Tully.
- Utt, a septon and member of the Brave Companions mercenary company.

V

- Lady Vaith
- Val
- Valarr Targaryen
- Varamyr, called "Varamyr Six-skins". A wildling skinchanger.
- Vardis Egen, knight and Captain-of-guards at the Eyrie.
- Vargo Hoat, captain of the Brave Companions, a sellsword company. A Qohorik. Known for hacking limbs (typically hands and feet) off captives.
- Varly
- Varys
- Vayon Poole, steward to Winterfell and House Stark
- Vickon Greyjoy
- Victarion Greyjoy
- Visenya Targaryen
- Viserys Targaryen

- Vulture King
- Vylarr
- Vyman

W

- Walda Frey, called "Fat Walda"
- Walda Frey, called "Fair Walda"
- Walda Rivers
- Walder Frey, called "Big Walder". A ward of Winterfell.
- Walder Frey, called "Black Walder"
- Walder Frey, called "Little Walder". A ward of Winterfell.
- Walder Frey, called "Red Walder"
- Walder Frey, called "The Late Lord Frey". Lord of the Crossing.
- Walder Rivers, called "Bastard Walder"
- Wallen
- Walton Frey
- Walton Stark
- Walton, called "Steelshanks." Captain of Roose Bolton's guards.
- Waltyr Frey
- Warren
- Watty
- Waymar Royce]].
- Wayn
- Weasel
- The Weeper, an infamous wildling raider.
- Weese, servant overseer at Harrenhal. A soldier in the service of Ser Gregor Clegane.
- Wenda
- Wendamyr, a Maester in service on Pyke.
- Wendel Manderly, second son of Lord Wyman Manderly.
- Wendello Qar Deeth
- Werlag
- Wex Pyke, squire to Prince Theon Greyjoy.
- Whalen Frey
- Whitesmile Wat, a singer.
- Wilbert, the Knight of Stoney Sept.
- Wilbert "Little Lion" Osgrey, marshall of the Northmarch at the time of Gyles the Green. Killed by Lancel Lannister.

- Wild Wyl Waynwood, slain by Daemon Blackfyre on the Redgrass Field.
- Will, called "Hookface". a guard at Dragonstone
- Will, a ranger of the Night's Watch.
- Willamen
- Willas Tyrell
- Willem Darry, master-at-arms for the Red Keep. Targaryen loyalist that smuggled Viserys and Daenerys Targaryen out of Westeros at the end of the War of the Usurper.
- Willem Lannister, squire to Ser Jaime Lannister.
- William Stark
- Willis Wode.
- Willit
- Willum
- Woth
- Wyl
- Wylis Manderly, a knight and heir to White Harbour.
- Wylla
- Wyman Manderly, Lord of White Harbour.
- Wynton Stout, an elderly knight of the Night's Watch.

XYZ

- Xaro Xhoan Daxos, a merchant prince of Qarth.
- Ygritte, a red-haired wildling woman said to be lucky and kissed by fire. Jon Snow's consort. Killed during the wildling attack on the Wall.
- Yohn Royce, called "Bronze Yohn". Lord of Runestone.
- Yoren, senior "Wandering Crow" or recruiter for the Night's Watch. Killed during battle with Ser Amory Lorch's forces.
- Lord Yronwood, Warden of the Boneway, The Bloodroyal. Died from wounds taken in a duel with Oberyn Martell.
- Zollo, called "Fat Zollo". A Dothraki sellsword and member the Brave Companions mercenary company.

Article Sources and Contributors

A Song of Ice and Fire *Source*: http://en.wikipedia.org/?oldid=390188855 *Contributors*: 1 anonymous edits

George R. R. Martin *Source*: http://en.wikipedia.org/?oldid=389246827 *Contributors*: 1 anonymous edits

A Game of Thrones *Source*: http://en.wikipedia.org/?oldid=389861908 *Contributors*:

A Clash of Kings *Source*: http://en.wikipedia.org/?oldid=386088855 *Contributors*: 1 anonymous edits

A Storm of Swords *Source*: http://en.wikipedia.org/?oldid=390467605 *Contributors*: 1 anonymous edits

A Feast for Crows *Source*: http://en.wikipedia.org/?oldid=384812340 *Contributors*: 1 anonymous edits

A Dance with Dragons *Source*: http://en.wikipedia.org/?oldid=390435724 *Contributors*:

Tales of Dunk and Egg *Source*: http://en.wikipedia.org/?oldid=382359625 *Contributors*: Camileck

Game of Thrones (TV series) *Source*: http://en.wikipedia.org/?oldid=390344224 *Contributors*: 1 anonymous edits

List of characters in A Song of Ice and Fire *Source*: http://en.wikipedia.org/?oldid=386779109 *Contributors*: 1 anonymous edits

Image Sources, Licenses and Contributors

file:Georgerr.PNG *Source*: http://bibliocm.bibliolabs.com/mwAnon/index.php?title=File:Georgerr.PNG *License*: Public Domain *Contributors*: Bree Chan from New York City, United States

Image:George R. R. Martin.jpg *Source*: http://bibliocm.bibliolabs.com/mwAnon/index.php?title=File:George_R._R._Martin.jpg *License*: GNU Free Documentation License *Contributors*: Ausir, Winterkind

Image:GeorgeRRMartinCW98 wb.jpg *Source*: http://bibliocm.bibliolabs.com/mwAnon/index.php?title=File:GeorgeRRMartinCW98_wb.jpg *License*: GNU Free Documentation License *Contributors*: User:Elf

CPSIA information can be obtained at www.ICGtesting.com
Printed in the USA
239825LV00006B/90/P

9 781240 914616